I0759550

SIMPLY SPEEDY CHINESE

Simply Speedy Chinese

By Suzie Lee

Photography by
Uyen Luu

Meals in 30 Minutes or Less

Quadrille

INTRODUCTION

I grew up in a family of seven, with three older sisters and one younger brother, in Lisburn in Northern Ireland. Our mum and dad had established our popular family Chinese takeaway, Man Lee, in Ballymacash in 1980, and this is where we spent our childhoods. We all worked in the takeaway – starting with what was essentially a butter knife for chopping onions and building on our skills through the years, up to deveining prawns (shrimp) and using the fryers and woks.

I was surrounded by food 24/7 and, in Chinese culture, food and family are closely intertwined.

'*Lai toung mm toung ngaw*?' (Are you hungry?) is the first phrase we ask anyone who comes to our home!

I loved being in the kitchen with my mum in the takeaway and it was amazing to watch her create, cook and command a whole kitchen while also juggling mum life. She was superwoman!

My mum knew I loved cooking. She bought me *The Good Housekeeping Cookbook* when I was 15 and I cooked most of the recipes in it, as I loved learning. I wanted to go to cookery school in London after my GCSEs, but my mum passed away very suddenly on 8 February 2000 when I was 16, in my GCSE year.

After losing my mum, I had to become a 'mum' to my 15-year-old brother and 7-year-old cousin It was a real wake-up call. Cooking became a necessity, and I watched TV cookery programmes, read magazines and started to cook from my prized *Good Housekeeping* cookbook again. That time was like one big experiment, as I was finding my way in the kitchen.

I am very fortunate to have spent precious time going to cafés and restaurants with my mum during her last year, when my three big sisters were away at university. When my mum and I ate something we enjoyed, we would try to recreate it at home, which was a lot of fun. We often adapted the dishes, which made them slightly different and I am still experimental in my cooking – making the most of the ingredients I have and just rustling something up.

My mum is my inspiration. She was a self-taught cook and the head chef of our takeaway. I have always believed that things happen for a reason, however heartbreaking or difficult a situation might be. While I didn't end up going to cookery school – instead studying and later becoming a Chartered Accountant – I always kept cooking in the kitchen.

For a really long time, cooking Chinese food was not my go-to, but when I had my two children, the need to preserve my heritage and show my children their culture through food, just as my mum did for us, brought me back to it.

Being in the kitchen is my therapy and it is also a way to reconnect with my mum. Now, my children really enjoy helping me in the kitchen and we play together too – it is so important for them to feel comfortable in the kitchen, as fewer people today know how to cook or want to learn. I am trying to break this cycle.

In February 2020, I won the BBC's *Best Home Cook* and have since presented four seasons of my own TV show, called *Suzie Lee: Home Cook Hero* on BBC One. My latest TV show is *Suzie Lee's Great Food Made Simple*, in which I visit local chefs in their restaurants in Northern Ireland and create my version of their three-course meals. I also work with different organizations in Northern Ireland, running basic food-prep courses and targeted cooking workshops for easy meals, budget cooking with storecupboard essentials, healty snacks and family-led meals. When I think about where I am now on my food journey – with three cookbooks and five TV cookery shows in five years – well, humbled is an understatement.

My recipes are accessible and not restrictive, and the majority of the ingredients can be bought in your local supermarket. Cooking is all about practice, so taste each dish as you go and adjust it to your tastebuds (you'll be the one eating it, after all). If you want something to be saltier, add more salt or soy sauce. Trust your own palate.

For me, food is absolutely fundamental to family and social life, as it brings everyone together, crossing cultures and breaking down barriers. Eating together is a special time for people to sit down, chat, decompress and reconnect, while enjoying even the simplest of meals.

WHY SPEEDY?

Life is busy for everyone and balancing our different responsibilities can be difficult – with a young family of my own, this is something that I know all too well. I pride myself on being able to create quick, delicious and well-balanced meals, inspired by my mum's cooking and the dishes that I grew up eating.

Chinese cooking is all about the preparation – getting everything chopped and ready, then quickly cooking the final dish – so I have gathered together a range of recipes that use my favourite speedy hacks and tips and also make the most of what you already have in your cupboards, refrigerator and freezer (or that can be found easily in your local supermarkets).

People also reach out to me on social media, asking for the recipes for the dishes I've made over the years, so I have drawn on these for the book.

Part of my speedy strategy is that there should always be a protein, a carb and a vegetable in every meal I make

Making balanced meals is not as difficult as you may think – I always have broccoli, green beans and other vegetables on hand to quickly and easily increase the nutritional content of my meals and to make sure my children eat green veg every day. Reducing food waste is close to my heart, too, and using up leftovers and other ingredients you have to hand is a sure-fire way to not only cook more economically but also to make your mealtimes faster and fuss-free – no more hunting through cupboards or in specialist shops!

These are recipes that I make all the time and which have been part of my family's diet for years, from Beef Fried Rice (page 74) to Sweet Chilli Prawn Skewers (page 30) and Mango Pancakes (page 165).

Whatever you fancy, this book is stuffed with tasty recipes for dishes that are ready in minutes.

HOW TO USE THIS BOOK

The chapters in this book are organized according to the amount of time each recipe takes to prepare and cook: 10 minutes, 15 minutes, 20 minutes and 30 minutes. You can choose one dish depending on the time you have, or make multiple dishes at once to suit your mood. There is a vast range of dishes across the chapters, including snacks, rice dishes, noodles, chicken, beef, duck, pork, seafood and dessert.

STAPLE INGREDIENTS

SEASONINGS AND SPICES

Light and dark soy sauce
Toasted sesame oil
Oyster sauce or vegetarian/mushroom stir-fry sauce
Shaoxing wine
Rice vinegar
Black vinegar
Dried fermented black beans
Toban djan/doubanjiang (fermented chilli bean paste)
Fermented red and white tofu (bean curd)
Chilli crisp oil
Ketchup
Tomato purée (paste)
Sesame paste/tahini
Peanut butter
Chicken or vegetable stock powder and cubes
Caster (superfine) sugar
Granulated sugar
Soft brown sugar (light or dark)
Vanilla extract
Honey
Black treacle (molasses)
Hoisin sauce
XO sauce
Satay sauce paste
Fine sea salt
White pepper
Black pepper
Chinese five-spice powder
Garlic granules
Chilli (hot pepper) flakes
Star anise
Cinnamon sticks

STORECUPBOARD

Dried shiitake mushrooms
Sesame seeds (white, black or both)
Peanuts
Lap cheong (Chinese cured sausage)
Evaporated milk
Condensed milk
Coconut milk
Tinned mango
Rolled oats
Panko breadcrumbs
Basmati rice
Noodles (rice, egg, glass and udon)
Ready-to-use rice cakes
Cornflour (cornstarch)
Rice flour (plain and glutinous)
Plain (all-purpose) flour
Self-raising (self-rising) flour
Vegetable oil
Wheat starch
Spam
Corned beef
Pickled Chinese cabbage
Tofu (firm, medium and silken)
Orange cordial
Sweetcorn (tinned and creamed)

FRESH

Ginger root (fresh or frozen)
Onions
Garlic (fresh or frozen)
Spring onions (scallions)
Chillies
Vegetables, such as green beans, peas, broccoli, spinach, carrots, onions, courgettes (zucchini) and (bell) peppers
Tomatoes
Pineapple (fresh or canned)
Lemons
Oranges
Eggs
Milk

FROZEN

Wonton wrappers
Gyoza wrappers
Frozen vegetables
Quorn mince (TVP)
King prawns (shrimp)

MUST-HAVE EQUIPMENT

There are a few must-have items that will aid you on your speedy Chinese cooking journey, and which I therefore feel are worth the investment. These items are part and parcel of my daily cooking routine and make my life so much easier.

WOK

You do not have to buy an expensive non-stick wok. The key to making a stainless-steel, aluminium or cast-iron wok non-stick is to 'season' it. To do this, use some paper towels to rub vegetable or sunflower oil over the inside of the wok, so the whole surface has a light coating of oil. Heat the wok slowly on the stovetop until it is smoking and then wipe thoroughly with more paper towels. Repeat the oiling, heating and wiping process until the paper towel comes away clean. The wok will blacken and lose its silver colour. It is now seasoned, and you have given your wok '*wok hei*', which means 'energy' or 'breath' of the wok.

METAL SIEVE (STRAINER)

Use to strain noodles, blanch vegetables and remove excess food fragments from oil if deep-frying.

STEAMER

Steamer, or a large pan with a lid into which you can fit a trivet stand, steam rack or heatproof dish.

TONGS

Used to extract food from woks and pans and to mix and stir.

MEASURING JUG (PITCHER), SPOONS AND SCALES

These items are important for the precision required in the recipes.

KEY TECHNIQUES

I use some methods, terms and ingredients frequently throughout the book, so I have pulled them all together and explain them fully here.

CORNFLOUR (CORNSTARCH)

I love cornflour because it is such a versatile ingredient. It can be used in many different ways. These are the main techniques I use cornflour for:

Velveting: add cornflour to your meat marinade and then, as the meat cooks, the cornflour acts as a barrier, helping to keep moisture in and the meat juicy.

Binding: used to bind ingredients together in recipes such as Stuffed Steamed Tofu (page 86) and Quick Dumplings (page 110).

Crisping: used to help form a crispy exterior when deep- or pan-frying foods, such as Honey Chilli Beef (page 132).

Thickener: use this to create a paste for thickening soups and sauces. Cornflour paste (also called slurry) is the key sauce thickener in all Chinese cooking. It is made by combining cornflour and water at a ratio of 1:2. Mix 1 tablespoon of cold or cooled water with 1 tablespoon of cornflour in a bowl until fully combined. Do not use hot water, as this will create a lumpy mixture. Give the mixture a stir before using it, as the cornflour will have settled to the bottom of the bowl.

BLANCHING/PARBOILING MEAT

This is always done in Chinese cooking. Place the meat in a saucepan of cold water and bring it to the boil to allow the impurities to float to the surface. This helps reduce excess fat in the meat, removes blood from the bones and the taste of gaminess from the meat, as well as ensuring that any broth or soup you make with the meat will be very clear. I hate waste, so I don't actually throw away the water the meat was boiled in as it holds a lot of flavour. I just make sure the impurities and scum are skimmed off with a sieve (strainer) before using this liquid for soups or broths.

STEAMING

Steaming is a great way to cook vegetables, as it helps retain their nutrients. The steamer is also useful for cooking meat, fish and dumplings. If you do not have a steamer, I would highly recommend getting one, but you can also make a makeshift one with a pan and trivet (see equipment list opposite).

SPLASH OF WATER

Always add a splash of water to vegetables when you are stir-frying to stop them from catching and burning in the wok.

TIME-SAVING TIPS

1. Plan your meals at the beginning of each week, so you can organize your shopping list. Maybe even choose a day to meal prep, so you can be efficient in preparing your ingredients in advance. That way, they will be ready to use when you cook during the week.
2. Make sure you have a well-stocked cupboard. This will mean that you can make many of these dishes without having to buy very much else, as the key ingredients are used in countless recipes.
3. An air fryer has been a welcome addition to our household, both to speed up the cooking of some dishes but also so we can cook smaller quantities.
4. Use a food processor to blend, mix and grate in order to speed up the prep process.
5. Batch-cook and freeze dishes to save time and effort in the future. To reduce the spent time reheating a meal, divide the dishes into individual portions.
6. Use leftovers if you have them! There are a number of recipes in this book that utilize leftovers. Incorporating these ingredients not only saves you time but also reduces food waste.
7. Organizing your kitchen is essential. Ensuring you stock up often, store ingredients in a logical place and properly label them facilitates easy access. If you are batch-cooking, make sure you have enough containers to freeze the dishes and also space in your freezer.
8. The more you cook, the better you will get at multitasking, which will mean you become more productive and efficient.
9. Keep on top of your kitchen. Clean as you go because clearing the clutter and mess as you cook will help with post-meal cleaning.

10 MINUTES OR LESS

This chapter features some classic veggie dishes that are great for sharing, along with a few super-speedy snacks, like My Hot Chilli Fried Egg Sandwich (page 23), which is so simple but so tasty, and the easy-peasy Sweet Chilli Prawn Skewers (page 30), which I like to eat with flatbread, pickled veggies and salad. I have also included the iconic Satay Beef and Egg Sandwich (page 32), which you will find in every Hong Kong *cha chaan teng* (Westernized coffee shop).

There is minimal prep time for these dishes and each uses very few ingredients, making the most of larder and cupboard ingredients like eggs, vegetables, soy sauce, chilli crisp oil and oyster sauce.

CHAPTER ONE

My Hot Chilli Fried Egg Sandwich

This is my quick go-to lunch or snack. Nothing can beat a fried egg sandwich – especially when the egg has been fried in chilli crisp oil! I love this with freshly buttered bread.

Serves 1
Cook: 5 minutes

INGREDIENTS

1 teaspoon chilli crisp oil with crispy bits
1 large (US extra large) egg
2 slices of cooked chicken or ham
2 slices of bread of your choice, toasted if desired
handful of spinach (whole leaves or shredded)
butter, salted, for spreading

METHOD

1. Pour the chilli oil (without the crispy bits) into a frying pan over a medium heat and fry the egg for about 3 minutes until the white has cooked.
2. Add the crispy bits from the chilli oil and cook the egg for another minute or so, depending on how you like it cooked, then remove from the pan. I sometimes like to fry the chicken or ham in the same frying pan as the egg for 30–60 seconds to heat through.
3. Butter the bread or toast, then assemble your sandwich, starting with the egg, then the ham or chicken (or both) and the spinach.

Stir-fried Choi Sum

When I was growing up, vegetables were always part of every meal. My mum and my aunties always told us, '*sik choi!*' (eat vegetables) at mealtimes! Chinese culture places great importance on eating vegetables due to their nutritional benefits.

Serves 3–4
Prep: 1 minute
Cook: 5 minutes

INGREDIENTS

300 g (10½ oz) *choi sum* (Chinese flowering cabbage), stalks chopped into 5–7.5 cm (2–3 in) pieces, leaves left whole
½ tablespoon vegetable oil
2 garlic cloves, finely chopped
2 tablespoons light soy sauce
pinch of ground white pepper
1 teaspoon sesame oil

METHOD

1. Bring a wok or saucepan of water to the boil and blanch the *choi sum* for 1 minute, then drain.
2. Place the wok or pan back over a high heat, add the vegetable oil and garlic, and fry for about 1 minute until just golden.
3. Add the soy sauce and white pepper and allow to simmer for another minute.
4. Add the *choi sum*, toss it through the sauce and cook for another minute, then drizzle with the sesame oil and serve.

Chilli Crisp Green Beans

Green beans are eaten at least four times a week in our household! I keep coming up with different ways to cook them because we love them so much. This recipe is one of my favourite quick-and-easy options.

Serves 2–3
Prep: 1 minute
Cook: 5 minutes

INGREDIENTS

200 g (7 oz) green beans, topped and tailed
2 teaspoons dark soy sauce
2 teaspoons chilli crisp oil

METHOD

1. Bring a wok or saucepan of water to the boil and blanch the green beans for 1 minute, then drain.
2. Place the wok or pan back over a high heat and add the soy sauce and chilli oil. Cook for 30–60 seconds until caramelized.
3. Add the green beans and toss them through the sauce, then serve.

Stir-fried Lettuce with Garlic

When Mum was running low on the usual green vegetables like broccoli or green beans, she would rustle up this dish for us – heaven forbid we would have a dinner without green veg! Iceberg lettuce was always in stock at our takeaway because it was the garnish to many of our dishes. So, never fear, we always had a plate of veggies to eat! This commitment to serving greens with every meal is something I have adopted with my own children. This recipe is super quick – you just have to blanch the lettuce and drizzle over the sauce. It is simply delicious!

Serves 4
Prep: 5 minutes
Cook: 5 minutes

INGREDIENTS

2 tablespoons vegetable oil
2 garlic cloves, finely sliced
1 iceberg lettuce, cored, leaves separated and any large leaves torn in half
2 heaped tablespoons oyster sauce
1 tablespoon light soy sauce

METHOD

1. Heat the oil in a wok over a high heat, then fry the garlic for about 2 minutes until golden.
2. Remove the garlic slices and set aside, then pour enough water for blanching into the wok and bring to the boil.
3. Blanch the lettuce leaves quickly until just wilted, then strain, reserving the water. Place the leaves in a dish.
4. Combine the oyster sauce, soy sauce and a ladleful of the blanching water in a small saucepan, mix well and bring to the boil for 2 minutes.
5. Drizzle the sauce over the lettuce, then sprinkle over the garlic slices.

Sweet Chilli Prawn Skewers

This is a super-quick and tasty dish that I came up with one day for lunch. We love prawns (shrimp) in our house. I like serving them on a homemade flatbread or tortilla wrap with some pickled veg, salad and a yoghurt dressing seasoned with some salt and pepper and a squeeze of lemon.

Serves 1
Prep: 5 minutes
Cook: 5 minutes

INGREDIENTS

75g (2½ oz) king prawns (jumbo shrimp), butterflied and digestive tract removed
½ teaspoon finely chopped garlic
½ teaspoon chilli oil (optional)
1 teaspoon finely chopped red chilli
1 tablespoon honey
large pinch of fine sea salt
pinch of ground white pepper

TIP

If using wooden skewers, make sure to soak them in water for at least 30 minutes beforehand to stop them from burning or charring.

METHOD

1. Mix together the prawns, garlic, chilli oil, chopped chilli, honey and salt and white pepper in a bowl. Leave to marinate for 5 minutes.
2. Preheat the grill (broiler) until it reaches its highest setting.
3. Thread the prawns onto skewers or simply place them on a sheet of foil on the grill tray.
4. Grill for 5–6 minutes until the prawns are cooked through, flipping them halfway through, then serve.

Satay Beef and Egg Sandwich

Cha chaan tengs are cafés in Hong Kong that serve up Western versions of Cantonese dishes. This iconic beef dish can be served in a bap or sandwich bread, or on rice or noodles. I also like to serve mine with Chinese-style Scrambled Eggs (page 39). The satay beef is so soft and tasty that it is delicious whatever way it's served.

Serves 2
Prep: 5 minutes
Cook: 5 minutes

INGREDIENTS

250 g (9 oz) beef rump (sirloin) steak, fat trimmed and steak finely sliced against the grain
2½ teaspoons cornflour (cornstarch)
2 large (US extra large) eggs, seasoned with a pinch of salt and pepper
small pinch of chicken stock powder
2 tablespoons vegetable oil
3½ tablespoons water, plus extra as needed
1 tablespoon satay paste (adjust the quantity to your preferred spice level)
½ heaped tablespoon peanut butter (smooth or crunchy)
large pinch of caster (superfine) sugar
½ teaspoon garlic granules
1 teaspoon sesame oil
ground white pepper

TO SERVE

4 slices of white bread, toasted
unsalted butter, for spreading

METHOD

1. Combine the beef strips with a teaspoon of cornflour in a bowl and toss to lightly coat the beef.
2. In a separate bowl, whisk together the eggs, chicken stock powder, a teaspoon of vegetable oil, the remaining cornflour and 1½ tablespoons of water. Set to one side.
3. Heat a wok or frying pan over a high heat and add a tablespoon of vegetable oil. Fry the beef strips for about 2 minutes until just cooked, then push to one side of the pan.
4. Add the satay paste, peanut butter, sugar, garlic granules, sesame oil and remaining water to the other side of the wok or pan and stir to combine. Allow to bubble for a couple of minutes, then toss everything together in the pan. Season to taste – I like a good kick of white pepper.
5. Cook for a further 2 minutes, then add another splash of water if you want the satay beef saucier.
6. In a separate pan, add half a tablespoon of vegetable oil over a high heat and add the egg mixture. Immediately turn the heat down to medium and, using a spatula, push the eggs from the edges of the pan to the middle. You want soft, just cooked, eggs, which will take approximately 2 minutes.
7. Serve the satay beef and egg on toasted, buttered bread.

Vitasoy
Vitasoy

15 MINUTES OR LESS

The recipes in this chapter require a little more prep time, but with this comes a huge variety of dishes, including snacks, vegetables, noodles, rice and salads. The Mini Steamed Eggs with Spring Onions (page 52) are a highlight for me – they remind me of my mum and are the ultimate comfort food: silky smooth and just delicious with a bowl of rice.

CHAPTER TWO

Chinese-style Scrambled Eggs

These are scrambled eggs with a twist! The chicken stock powder adds extra flavour and the cornflour (cornstarch) paste gives the eggs a lovely fluffy texture.

Serves 4
Prep: 5 minutes
Cook: 10 minutes

INGREDIENTS

4 medium (US large) eggs
1 tablespoon plus 1 teaspoon vegetable oil
large pinch of chicken stock powder
1 tablespoon cornflour (cornstarch) mixed with 3 tablespoons water to make a paste
1 spring onion (scallion), chopped into 1 cm (½ in) pieces

METHOD

1. Beat the eggs in a bowl with 1 teaspoon of the vegetable oil, the chicken stock powder and cornflour paste until light and bubbly. Add the chopped spring onions and mix again.
2. Heat a wok over a high heat and add the remaining tablespoon of vegetable oil, then pour in the egg mixture. Reduce the heat to medium. The eggs should bubble rapidly around the edges. Cook for about 30 seconds, then use a spatula to scoop the egg mixture off the bottom of the wok and fold it on top of itself. This will allow the uncooked egg to fill the bottom of the wok. Repeat this fold twice, then remove the wok from the heat.
3. Keep folding the egg on top of itself until the residual heat from the wok has cooked the eggs. If it doesn't, place the wok back over a high heat again and allow the egg to cook without moving the mixture (but if it starts to burn, fold again). Serve.

Fried Salted Peanuts

Nuts are consumed in vast quantities in our household, and we love flavoured ones. We also love the simple toasted nuts you get in Chinese restaurants as a snack in the middle of the table with pickled vegetables. They are so moreish. The strained oil can be used for cooking other dishes and is also great for making chilli crisp oil.

Serves 4
Prep: 5 minutes
Cook: 10 minutes

INGREDIENTS

200 ml (7 fl oz/scant 1 cup) vegetable oil
200 g (7 oz/1¼ cups) skin-on raw peanuts (red peanuts)
fine sea salt

METHOD

1. Put the oil and peanuts in a wok over a low heat and slowly increase the heat to medium, stirring often. You want to cook the peanuts through, not just heat the outside.
2. Cook the peanuts over a medium heat for 6–8 minutes until you start to hear them popping, then immediately remove the wok from the heat. You don't want to burn them!
3. Strain the nuts through a metal colander or sieve (strainer) set over a bowl to catch the oil.
4. Sprinkle the nuts with a generous pinch of salt and toss well. Enjoy slightly cooled or cold.
5. Store in an airtight jar for up to a week.

Smashed Cucumber Salad

This is an easy, tasty and addictive salad that is tangy with ginger and garlic and has an umami kick from the soy sauce. It's a very yummy salad that doesn't need any extra explanation!

Serves 2
Prep: 15 minutes

INGREDIENTS

1 cucumber, topped and tailed
1 teaspoon fine sea salt
1 teaspoon grated fresh ginger root
½ teaspoon grated garlic
3 teaspoons light soy sauce
2 teaspoons rice vinegar
1 teaspoon sesame oil
freshly ground black pepper

METHOD

1. Cut the cucumber in half lengthways, then bash it with a rolling pin, mallet or bottle and chop it roughly into chunks.
2. Put the cucumber pieces in a colander or sieve (strainer), sprinkle over the salt and toss through. Leave for 15 minutes to allow the liquid to drain, then squeeze the cucumber to remove any remaining liquid.
3. Put the ginger and garlic in a large jar or airtight container, add the soy sauce, vinegar, sesame oil and a good crack of black pepper. Shake to combine, then add the cucumber and shake again.
4. Serve straight away or chill in the refrigerator, where the salad will keep until the following day.

Stir-fried Morning Glory with Fermented Tofu

Mum used to make this dish - called *fu yu tung choi* - all the time when I was younger, and now I love ordering it at restaurants. The addition of fermented tofu (bean curd) adds layers of flavour to this dish.

Serves 4
Prep: 5 minutes
Cook: 10 minutes

INGREDIENTS

400 g (14 oz) morning glory (water spinach), stalks trimmed and chopped into 7.5 cm (3 in) pieces, leaves left whole
2 tablespoons vegetable oil
10 g (½ oz) fresh ginger root, cut into 4 thin slices
2 garlic cloves, sliced
½ red chilli, sliced (optional; add more if you like food spicier), plus extra to serve
2 large lumps of white fermented tofu (bean curd) (about 20 g/¾ oz)
1 tablespoon water
1½ tablespoons Shaoxing wine
fine sea salt and ground white pepper

METHOD

1. Soak the morning glory in water for 5 minutes, then rinse under running water to remove any excess soil or debris. Drain.
2. Heat the oil in a wok over a high heat and fry the ginger, garlic and chilli (if using) for about 1 minute until fragrant.
3. Add the fermented tofu and water and mash with a wooden spoon or spatula to create a milky-looking liquid.
4. Increase the heat to the highest setting and add the morning glory stalks, then toss them in the liquid for about 1 minute. Cover and steam for 2 minutes on the high heat.
5. Add the morning glory leaves and toss through for about 1 minute, then cover again and steam for another minute.
6. Add the Shaoxing wine around the edge of the pan, so it sizzles on the metal, then toss through. Add a large pinch of salt and white pepper. Taste and adjust the seasoning if needed.
7. Serve garnished with more sliced chilli (if using).

Sweet and Hot Stir-fried Aubergines and Courgettes

Some of the recipes in this book only require a small amount of one ingredient. So, here is a great recipe for using up leftover aubergines (eggplants) and courgettes (zucchini)! Chop them up into similar-sized pieces, then add the other easy-to-source ingredients and fry them all together to create this deliciously garlicky, sweet and hot veggie dish. Try this with hot basmati rice or as a side on its own – it's very addictive!

Serves 2
Prep: 5 minutes
Cook: 10 minutes

INGREDIENTS

1 tablespoon vegetable oil
1 teaspoon finely chopped garlic
1 small aubergine (eggplant), cut into cubes (about 500 g/1 lb 2 oz)
1 courgette (zucchini), cut into cubes (about 500 g/1 lb 2 oz)
2 tablespoons *toban djan* (fermented chilli bean paste), or to taste
2 heaped tablespoons honey
fine sea salt and freshly ground white pepper

METHOD

1. Heat the oil in a wok over a high heat and fry the garlic for about 1 minute until fragrant.
2. Add the aubergine and courgette and fry for about 5 minutes until golden, stirring continuously so that they don't burn.
3. Add the *toban djan* and fry for 1 minute, then add the honey and allow it to bubble for another couple of minutes until everything has caramelized.

Season to taste, then serve.

Steamed Pak Choi with Garlic and Oyster Sauce

I am a big fan of Asian vegetables – and there are so many to choose from. I grew up eating pak choi (bok choy) in copious amounts in many different dishes.

Serves 4
Prep: 2 minutes
Cook: 10 minutes

INGREDIENTS

3 large pak choi (bok choy), bottom part sliced off and then quartered lengthways
1 teaspoon vegetable oil
1 teaspoon finely chopped garlic
1 tablespoon oyster sauce
100 ml (3½ fl oz/scant ½ cup) water
1 teaspoon cornflour (cornstarch) mixed with 2 teaspoons water to make a paste

METHOD

1. Prepare a steamer, then place the pak choi in the steamer in one layer and steam for 6–7 minutes until just cooked.
2. While the pak choi is steaming, make the sauce. Heat the oil in a small saucepan over a medium heat and fry the garlic for 1 minute until fragrant. Add the oyster sauce, water and cornflour paste and stir until smooth. Now increase the heat to high and keep stirring until the sauce becomes glossy and thick.
3. Once the pak choi has steamed, place it on a plate, drizzle over the sauce and enjoy!

Cauliflower Stir-fry

This is a delicious, quick-and-easy stir-fry with staples I always have to hand – onions, carrots, and broccoli – and when cauliflower is in season, I throw that in, too. This particular stir-fry has become a regular feature in our household. It is light, fresh and highly nutritious.

Serves 4
Prep: 5 minutes
Cook: 10 minutes

INGREDIENTS

1 small broccoli, cut into florets
½ large cauliflower, cut into florets
1 tablespoon vegetable oil
1 large onion, diced
1 large carrot, peeled and sliced into thin rounds
1 tablespoon water
1 heaped tablespoon finely chopped fresh ginger root
2 large garlic cloves, finely chopped
2 heaped tablespoons oyster sauce
1½ tablespoons light soy sauce
½ teaspoon vegetable or chicken stock powder or ½ stock cube, crumbled
250 ml (8 fl oz/1 cup) hot water
1 teaspoon sesame oil
1 tablespoon cornflour (cornstarch) mixed with 2 tablespoons water to make a paste
fine sea salt and freshly ground white pepper

TO SERVE

sliced spring onions (scallions)
rice or noodles

METHOD

1. Prepare a steamer, then place the broccoli and cauliflower florets in the steamer and steam for 6–7 minutes until they are just cooked. If you like cauliflower soft, then cook for another couple of minutes.
2. Heat the oil in a wok or large frying pan over a high heat, then add the onion and carrot and the water – this helps to soften the onions. Cook for 1 minute.
3. Add the ginger and garlic and fry for a further 2 minutes until aromatic.
4. Add the oyster sauce and soy sauce and cook for a couple of minutes, then add the stock powder or cube and water and simmer for another 2 minutes.
5. Now add the sesame oil, taste and then adjust the seasoning if required. If you prefer a thicker sauce, reduce the heat, then add the cornflour paste, increase the heat and stir until thickened. (If you like more sauce, just add more stock and cornflour paste.)
6. Add the cauliflower and broccoli, quickly toss everything together until coated in the sauce, then cook for another couple of minutes. Sprinkle with the spring onions and serve with rice or noodles.

Mini Steamed Eggs with Spring Onions

This is a very nostalgic dish for me, as it is one that Mum used to make. It can be easily transformed by adding other ingredients, such as prawns (shrimp), minced (ground) beef, minced pork, mushrooms and various types of vegetables. The silky-smooth eggs are steamed, which creates a texture not unlike a savoury custard. I happily eat this on its own but it is also great as a side dish.

Serves 2
Prep: 5 minutes
Cook: 10 minutes

INGREDIENTS

3 medium (US large) eggs, as fresh as possible
200 ml (7 fl oz/scant 1 cup) water
1 teaspoon chicken stock powder or 1 chicken stock cube, crumbled
good pinch of ground white pepper
1 teaspoon light soy sauce

TO SERVE

finely sliced spring onion (scallion) greens
drizzle of sesame oil

METHOD

1. Prepare a steamer.
2. Beat the eggs, water, chicken stock powder or cube and white pepper together in a jug (pitcher) until well combined (but try not to create too many air bubbles on top).
3. Place a small sieve (strainer) over a ramekin and pour half the egg mixture through it. This will collect any thick bits of egg and also help to break down some of the air bubbles. Repeat with a second ramekin.
4. Cover each ramekin tightly with cling film (plastic wrap) to stop the eggs getting mottled by condensation.
5. Place the ramekins in the steamer and steam for 10 minutes until they wobble when you jiggle them. Remove the ramekins from the steamer.
6. Remove the cling film and, using a knife, score a criss-cross pattern on top of the steamed eggs. Pour over the soy sauce, sprinkle with some spring onions and drizzle with sesame oil, then serve.

Fridge-raid Stir-fry

A lot of my cooking creations are accidental because I love to rustle up dishes using whatever ingredients I have at home. Combining bits and pieces to make something new is a win-win for me and this recipe is no different.

Serves 2
Prep: 5 minutes
Cook: 10 minutes

INGREDIENTS

1 large carrot, peeled and sliced on the diagonal
1 onion, chopped
1 celery stalk, sliced on the diagonal
1 red/yellow/orange (bell) pepper, diced
1 courgette (zucchini), cut into half-moons
1 tablespoon vegetable oil
2 teaspoons finely chopped garlic
2 tablespoons light soy sauce
1 teaspoon sesame oil
pinch of ground white pepper
pinch of caster (superfine) sugar

METHOD

1. Bring a saucepan of water to the boil and blanch the carrot, onion and celery for 1 minute, then drain and set aside.
2. Next, heat the oil in a wok over a high heat and fry the garlic, pepper and courgette for 1 minute until fragrant, then add the soy sauce and sesame oil.
3. Add the carrot, onion and celery to the wok and stir-fry until they are starting to caramelize, which will take approximately 2 minutes. Cook for another couple of minutes, season with white pepper and sugar then serve.

Hot Peanut Butter Noodles

This is one of my go-to easy meals for one. Quick, delicious, spicy and lip-smacking noodles, made using ingredients from the cupboard, so it is super easy! I like to eat this with a crispy fried egg, some fried peanuts, spring onions (scallions) and an extra drizzle of chilli oil.

Serves 1
Prep: 5 minutes
Cook: 10 minutes

INGREDIENTS

100 g (3½ oz) nest of dried thick egg noodles
1 heaped tablespoon peanut butter (crunchy or smooth)
1 teaspoon chilli crisp oil
½ teaspoon chicken or vegetable stock powder
1½ teaspoons rice vinegar (or more if you like it tangier)
drizzle of sesame oil

TO SERVE (OPTIONAL)

fried egg
Fried Salted Peanuts (page 40)
sliced spring onions (scallions)

METHOD

1. Bring a saucepan of water to the boil and cook the noodles according to the instructions on the packet.
2. In a serving bowl, combine the peanut butter, chilli crisp oil, stock powder and rice vinegar. Stir well to combine.
3. Once the noodles are cooked, add 1–2 tablespoons of the hot noodle cooking water to the bowl and stir to create a sauce.
4. Drain the noodles and add them to the bowl, then toss everything together until combined. Drizzle with sesame oil, then add any optional toppings and serve.

Duck and Silver Pin Noodle Soup

There was great debate in my family about how these noodles were served to us when we were younger. It was so long ago since we all ate them that no one had a definitive answer. We each remembered something different – the soup bowl version, the stir-fried version . . . So, I decided to make a recipe up myself and go with super-classic flavours in a light broth with one of my favourite meats – duck!

Serves 1
Prep: 5 minutes
Cook: 10 minutes

INGREDIENTS

1 duck breast, trimmed of excess fat and skin, then finely sliced
1 tablespoon vegetable oil
30 g (1 oz) fresh ginger root, finely sliced
1 large garlic clove, finely sliced
3 spring onions (scallions), chopped into 5 cm (2 in) pieces, white and green parts separated
2 tablespoons Shaoxing wine
250 ml (8 fl oz/1 cup) water
1 teaspoon chicken stock powder or 1 chicken stock cube, crumbled
1 x quantity Silver Pin Noodles (page 121) or 200 g (7 oz) udon noodles or rice cakes, cooked
fine sea salt and ground white pepper

TO SERVE

drizzle of sesame oil
blanched or steamed greens of your choice

METHOD

1. Season the duck to taste with salt and white pepper.
2. Heat the oil in a wok over a high heat and fry the sliced duck for 2 minutes, then transfer to a bowl and set aside. Do not clean the wok.
3. Add the ginger, garlic and white spring onions and cook for about 1 minute until aromatic. Add the Shaoxing wine and stir to deglaze. Next, add the water and chicken stock powder or cube and boil for 5 minutes. Add the spring onion greens.
4. Place the cooked noodles or rice in a bowl, then add the duck. Pour over the broth and drizzle with sesame oil. Add some blanched or steamed greens of your choice and serve.

Ketchup Fried Rice

My son LOVES ketchup and I love making fried rice, so this dish is our perfect combination. I was first inspired to make it after seeing someone create something similar online – I thought I would give the recipe a go, but I also decided to pack it with veggies and to use something that is usually discarded, like a broccoli stalk (I'm always thinking like a mummy!). The ketchup added a lovely tangy flavour to the dish.

Serves 2
Prep: 5 minutes
Cook: 10 minutes

INGREDIENTS

1 tablespoon vegetable oil
2 medium (US large) eggs, beaten
250 g (9 oz) Spam, diced into small cubes
1 teaspoon grated garlic
1 small carrot, peeled and grated
1 broccoli stalk, grated
250 g (9 oz/generous 1⅓ cups) cooked and cooled basmati rice (or a microwavable pouch)
1½ tablespoons light soy sauce
3 tablespoons ketchup, or to taste
small handful of frozen peas
small handful of sweetcorn, fresh, tinned or frozen
1 teaspoon sesame oil
fine sea salt and freshly ground white pepper

METHOD

1. Heat the oil in a wok over a high heat and then add the eggs. Cook for 2 minutes by swirling the wok every 15 seconds, so the uncooked egg fills the gaps, creating a lightly cooked omelette. Transfer the omelette to a plate. Do not clean the wok.
2. Now add the Spam to the wok and fry for a couple of minutes until it starts to colour. Add the garlic, carrot and broccoli stalk and sweat for 3 minutes.
3. Add the rice to the wok and break it down with a wooden spoon to get rid of any clumps, then pour over the soy sauce and ketchup. Keep stirring until the rice is uniform in colour and the sauce has been evenly distributed. Season to taste, adding more ketchup if you want the dish tangier.
4. Return the omelette to the wok, using the wooden spoon to break it up into bite-size pieces. This will take about 3 minutes.
5. Stir through the peas and sweetcorn, cooking for a minute or so until the vegetables are heated through, then pour the sesame oil around the edge of the wok and toss to combine before serving.

Curried Pineapple Fried Rice

This is a simple way to add more flavour and texture to your fried rice by incorporating pineapple and curry powder. The rice is fruity, but the curry flavour balances it really well.

Serves 2
Prep: 5 minutes
Cook: 10 minutes

INGREDIENTS

1 tablespoon vegetable oil
1 teaspoon finely chopped garlic
1 small onion, diced (any onion is fine – I used a red onion as I liked the pop of colour and flavour)
1 heaped tablespoon curry powder (mild, medium or hot)
1 carrot, peeled and diced
handful of frozen peas
2 spring onions (scallions), chopped into small pieces
250 g (9 oz/generous 1⅓ cups) cooked and cooled basmati rice (or a microwavable pouch)
2 tablespoons light soy sauce
200 g (7 oz) fresh pineapple, diced

METHOD

1. Heat a wok over a high heat and add the oil. Fry the garlic and onion for about 2 minutes until fragrant and slightly coloured. If the garlic and onion start to catch, add a splash of water.
2. Now add the curry powder and fry for another minute. Beware: the kitchen might get smoky at this point, so start the extractor fan.
3. Add the carrot, peas, spring onions, rice, soy sauce and pineapple. Toss everything together and break down the rice with a wooden spoon until it is uniform in colour, then fry for about 5 minutes.
4. Taste and adjust the seasoning, then serve.

XO Fried Rice

XO sauce was invented in Hong Kong by a chef at the Peninsula Hotel in the 1980s. Even though it is named after a Cognac, it doesn't have a drop of alcohol in it! The sauce was actually named to reflect the luxurious seafood products used to make it, like dried scallops and prawns (shrimp). XO sauce is one of those secret ingredients that I think people need to know about – it has a strong umami kick and it is so versatile, not just as a condiment but also to cook with. You can mix up the veggies in this dish, cook it without vegetables or, for more flavour and protein, add prawns or chicken.

Serves 2
Prep: 5 minutes
Cook: 10 minutes

INGREDIENTS

1 large tablespoon XO sauce (a mixture of oil and sediment), plus extra to serve
½ small onion, finely sliced
½ carrot, peeled and grated
½ small courgette (zucchini), grated
250 g (9 oz/generous 1⅓ cups) cooked and cooled basmati rice (or a microwavable pouch)
1 teaspoon light soy sauce
splash of sesame oil (optional)
2 teaspoons oil from the top of the XO sauce or vegetable oil
2 medium (US large) eggs
fine sea salt and ground white pepper
sliced spring onions (scallions), to serve

METHOD

1. Heat a wok over a high heat, then add the XO sauce. Quickly add the onion, carrot and courgette and cook for a couple of minutes.
2. Now add the rice and use a wooden spoon to break down any lumps, then add the soy sauce and mix well. Add the sesame oil (if using) and cook for a further 3 minutes until the moisture has evaporated and you can hear the rice and vegetables sizzling.
3. Meanwhile, heat the XO oil or vegetable oil in a small frying pan over a medium heat and fry the eggs to your liking.
4. Divide the rice between plates, top with the eggs and garnish with spring onions or more XO sauce.

XO

Suzie's Chicken and Pomelo Salad

I love pomelo – it is a grapefruit-like fruit that I grew up eating. I didn't know it was an exotic fruit until I was doing my own shopping aged 16 and realized you could only get them in Asian supermarkets at that time. I like to have a salad every day, and this habit drove me to develop a way of incorporating this fruit into one of them.

Serves 2
Prep time: 15 minutes

INGREDIENTS

1 tablespoon rice vinegar
1 tablespoon light soy sauce
1 tablespoon honey
1 teaspoon sesame oil
½ small red onion, finely sliced
1 large carrot, peeled and cut into thin julienne strips
½ small red cabbage, finely shredded
250 g (9 oz) cooked chicken, sliced or shredded
150–200 g (5½–7 oz) pomelo segments, broken up into smaller pieces
2–3 handfuls of spinach (shredded or whole leaves)
fine sea salt and freshly ground black pepper

METHOD

1. First, make the dressing in a large mixing bowl. Combine the rice vinegar, soy sauce, honey, sesame oil, a couple of cracks of black pepper, a good pinch of sea salt and the onion, mix well and leave to marinate for at least 10 minutes. This helps to reduce the raw flavour of the onions and makes them more mellow.
2. Now add the remaining ingredients, toss together and enjoy!

Sweet and Sour Sauce

Sweet and sour sauce is one of the most frequently requested sauce recipes. You can add it to so many things and it is delicious as a dipping sauce or drizzled over fried rice.

Makes about 500 ml (17 fl oz/ generous 2 cups)

INGREDIENTS

250 ml (8 fl oz/1 cup) water
110 g (4 oz/½ cup) granulated sugar
115 g (4¼ oz/½ cup) tomato purée (paste)
125 ml (4 fl oz/½ cup) clear, distilled vinegar
1–2 tablespoons cornflour (cornstarch) paste (see page 17) (optional)

METHOD

1. Add the water and sugar to a saucepan over a low heat and let the sugar dissolve.
2. Once the sugar has dissolved, add the tomato purée and vinegar. Let the mixture bubble away but keep stirring it to get rid of all the lumps. Bring the sauce to the boil and let it caramelize for a couple of minutes.
3. If you want a thicker sauce, reduce the heat, add the cornflour paste and stir it through. Bring the sauce to a boil and then simply cook until thickened.

Satay Sauce

Satay sauce is a unique peanut-based curry sauce, and a real favourite. The heat level can be dialled up by using a spicier curry powder or depending on the type of chilli you use.

Makes about 500 ml (17 fl oz/ generous 2 cups)

INGREDIENTS

1 tablespoon vegetable oil
1 small onion, finely diced
1½ tablespoons curry powder
½ large chilli, deseeded and finely chopped
1½ heaped tablespoons smooth peanut butter
1½ tablespoons soft dark brown soft sugar
½ teaspoon vegetable stock powder or ½ vegetable stock cube, crumbled
200 ml (7 fl oz/scant 1 cup) coconut milk
250 ml (8 fl oz/1 cup) water
1 teaspoon sesame oil
1–2 tablespoons cornflour (cornstarch) paste (see page 17) (optional)
fine sea salt and ground white pepper

METHOD

1. Heat the oil in a wok over a medium heat and fry the onion for a few minutes, then add the curry powder and fry for a minute. If the onion catches, add a splash of water.
2. Add the chilli, peanut butter, sugar and stock, simmer for a couple of minutes (the sauce will be very thick), then add the coconut milk and water. Season to taste. Add the sesame oil.
3. If you want a thicker sauce, reduce the heat, add the cornflour paste and stir through. Bring to a boil and cook until thickened (approximately 3–4 minutes). You may need to repeat this process until the sauce reaches your desired consistency.

Oyster Stir Fry Sauce

This is a sauce that uses the base of oyster sauce with added aromatics of ginger and garlic to make it even more fragrant and enhance your dishes still further.

Makes about 500 ml (17 fl oz/ generous 2 cups)

INGREDIENTS

1 tablespoon vegetable oil
1 teaspoon finely chopped fresh ginger root
1 heaped teaspoon finely chopped garlic
4 tablespoons oyster sauce
1 tablespoon light soy sauce
1 teaspoon chicken stock powder or 1 chicken stock cube, crumbled
1 teaspoon sesame oil
1–2 tablespoons cornflour (cornstarch) (optional) paste (see page 17)
fine sea salt and ground white pepper

METHOD

1. Heat the oil in a saucepan over a medium heat and fry the ginger and garlic for 1 minute until fragrant. Make sure they do not burn – if they start to catch, add a splash of water.
2. Add the oyster sauce, soy sauce and stock powder or cube and simmer for 5–6 minutes, then add the sesame oil. Season to taste.
3. If you want a thicker sauce, reduce the heat, add the cornflour paste and stir through. Bring to a boil and cook until thickened.

NOTE

If you aren't using these sauces straight away, once cooled, you can keep them in airtight containers in the refrigerator for up to five days. They can also be frozen for up to a month.

20 MINUTES OR LESS

With a little bit more time, this chapter lends itself to bigger sharing dishes, stir-fries, seafood dishes and, of course, fried rice and noodles, as well as two delicious and easy puddings, one steamed and one that requires no cooking at all.

CHAPTER THREE

Spring Onion Oil Noodles

My kids are generally indifferent to noodles, but when you make them crunchy and crispy, they are all over them. This is a basic chow mein recipe that I have jazzed up with spring onion (scallion) oil and then fried off in a disc shape until crisp.

Serves 2
Prep: 5 minutes
Cook: 15 minutes

INGREDIENTS

1 teaspoon fine sea salt
2 x 75 g (2¾ oz) nests of dried egg noodles
1 tablespoon light soy sauce
½ tablespoon dark soy sauce
1 tablespoon black vinegar
pinch of ground white pepper
sliced spring onions (scallions), to serve

FOR THE SPRING ONION OIL

6 spring onions (scallions), roughly chopped
100 ml (3½ fl oz/scant ½ cup) vegetable oil

METHOD

1. Bring a saucepan of water to the boil, add the salt and cook the noodles for 2 minutes. Drain and pat dry – the noodles should be dry to the touch. An absorbent dishcloth is great for this.
2. Next, make the spring onion oil. Put the spring onions and oil in a small saucepan over a medium heat and fry them for about 8 minutes until they are browned but not burned. Remove from the heat.
3. Remove the spring onions from the oil, discarding them, and then toss the noodles through the flavoured oil. Using tongs, remove the noodles from the oil and place in a bowl – if there is excess oil in the pan, you can store it in a small container to use another time. It will keep in the refrigerator for two weeks.
4. Now add the light soy sauce, dark soy sauce, black vinegar and white pepper to the bowl and toss to coat the noodles.
5. Heat a large, dry frying pan over a high heat and add the noodles. Stir-fry for about 2 minutes until some of the noodles have become charred, then press down with a plate to flatten them. Cook for a couple of minutes, then flip and repeat. Serve garnished with more spring onions.

Beef Fried Rice

This recipe evolved out of a need for something super speedy for my family that was also packed with lots of veggies and protein and made mostly from things I had to hand. Make sure whatever vegetables you choose are cut to the same size, so they cook evenly.

Serves 4
Prep: 10 minutes
Cook: 10 minutes

INGREDIENTS

2 tablespoons vegetable oil
4 medium (US large) eggs, beaten
1 onion, finely sliced
2 garlic cloves, finely chopped
40 g (1½ oz) fresh ginger root, finely sliced
2 teaspoons sesame oil, plus extra to taste
500 g (1 lb 2 oz) lean minced (ground) beef
1 medium carrot, peeled and grated
½ courgette (zucchini), grated
500 g (1 lb 2 oz/scant 3 cups) cooked and cooled basmati rice (or 2 microwavable pouches)
2 tablespoons light soy sauce, plus extra to taste
handful of frozen peas
2 tablespoons oyster sauce
fine sea salt and ground white pepper
sliced spring onions (scallions), to serve

METHOD

1. Heat 1 tablespoon of oil in a wok over a high heat and add the eggs. Cook for about 2 minutes, swirling the wok every 15 seconds, so the uncooked egg fills the gaps to create a lightly cooked omelette. Transfer the omelette to a plate. Do not clean the wok.
2. In the same wok, fry the onion until slightly soft (approximately 2–3 minutes), then add the garlic ginger and sesame oil and fry for 1 minute until fragrant.
3. Add the minced beef and fry for about 5 minutes.
4. Now add the carrot and courgette and toss for a couple of minutes.
5. Add the rice and break it down with a wooden spoon to remove any clumps, then add the soy sauce, omelette and peas and break the omelette into smaller pieces with the spoon.
6. Season to taste, then finish with the oyster sauce and some more soy sauce and sesame oil if needed. Garnish with spring onions before serving.

Chicken and Broccoli in Ginger and Garlic Sauce

Broccoli is a firm favourite in our house, so I make many, many dishes with it, including this one. Here, chicken and broccoli are cooked in a simple sauce made with chicken stock, ginger and garlic and thickened with cornstarch (cornflour). I love eating the broccoli stalks as well – they provide extra crunch and eating them helps to reduce food waste.

Serves 2
Prep: 5 minutes
Cook: 15 minutes

INGREDIENTS

250 g (9 oz) skinless and boneless chicken thighs or breast, cut into bite size pieces
1 teaspoon cornflour (cornstarch)
1 tablespoon oyster sauce
1 teaspoon sesame oil
pinch of fine sea salt, plus extra to taste
pinch of ground white pepper, plus extra to taste
½ broccoli, florets chopped into bite-size pieces and stalk cut into strips
1 tablespoon vegetable oil
½ teaspoon finely chopped garlic
½ teaspoon finely chopped fresh ginger root
2 teaspoons Shaoxing wine
1 teaspoon chicken stock powder or 1 chicken stock cube, crumbled
200 ml (7 fl oz/scant 1 cup) water mixed with 1 heaped teaspoon cornflour (cornstarch)
rice or noodles, to serve

METHOD

1. Combine the chicken, cornflour, oyster sauce, sesame oil and salt and white pepper in a bowl and set aside to marinate for at least 5 minutes.
2. Meanwhile, bring a saucepan of water to the boil and blanch the broccoli for around 1 minute, then drain.
3. Heat the vegetable oil in a wok or large frying pan over a high heat, add the marinated chicken and cook for 1–2 minutes on each side until lightly golden. Take the chicken out of the wok and set aside. Do not clean the wok.
4. Add the garlic and ginger to the wok and fry for 30–60 seconds until fragrant, then add the Shaoxing wine to deglaze the wok and cook for another minute.
5. Now add the chicken stock powder or cube, water and cornflour mixture, and stir well. Return the chicken to the pan and let it simmer away for 8–10 minutes, then add the broccoli and cook for a further 2 minutes. You can cook the broccoli for longer if you like it soft, but if you prefer it with a slight crunch, then stop cooking and it's ready to eat! Enjoy with rice or noodles.

TONES

Chicken and Spring Onion Stir-fry

Spring onions (scallions) are one of my favourite ingredients. They can be used in so many different ways - not just as a garnish but to cook with as well. This dish is packed with that delicious, fresh spring onion flavour.

Serves 4
Prep: 5 minutes
Cook: 15 minutes

INGREDIENTS

400 g (14 oz) skinless and boneless chicken thighs, finely sliced
1 teaspoon cornflour (cornstarch)
1 teaspoon oyster sauce
1 tablespoon vegetable oil, plus extra as needed
1 small white onion, sliced
4 spring onions (scallions), cut into 5 cm (2 in) pieces, white and green parts separated
1 heaped teaspoon finely chopped garlic
2 heaped teaspoons finely chopped fresh ginger root
1 teaspoon chicken stock powder or 1 chicken stock cube, crumbled
1 tablespoon dark soy sauce
150 ml (5 fl oz/scant ⅔ cup) water
1 teaspoon cornflour (cornstarch) mixed with 2 teaspoons of water to make a paste
1 teaspoon sesame oil

METHOD

1. Combine the chicken, cornflour and oyster sauce in a bowl and leave to marinate for about 5 minutes.
2. Heat a wok over a high heat, add the vegetable oil and fry the onion, the white parts of the spring onion, the garlic and ginger for 30–60 seconds until fragrant. If they start to catch, add a splash of water. Remove from the wok and set aside. Do not clean the wok.
3. Add another splash of oil to the wok and fry the marinated chicken pieces for a couple of minutes on each side until lightly golden.
4. Add the chicken stock powder or cube, soy sauce and water. Let this simmer away for 5–8 minutes until the chicken is just cooked.
5. If you want a thicker sauce, reduce the heat, add the cornflour paste and stir it through. Bring the sauce to a boil and cook until thickened.
6. Return the spring onion whites, onions, garlic and ginger to the wok and bubble for another minute or so, then toss in the spring onion greens. Drizzle the sesame oil around the edges of the wok and mix through. Serve.

Sticky Soy Sauce Salmon Rice Bowl

A salmon rice bowl is a go-to in our house. It is an easy dinner that changes every time I make it depending on the ingredients I have to hand. I keep the skin on the salmon fillets as it gives extra texture and because the skin holds additional nutrients.

Serves 2
Prep: 5 minutes
Cook: 15 minutes

INGREDIENTS

2 x 125 g (4½ oz) salmon fillets, skin on and cut into bite-size chunks
1 tablespoon honey
1 tablespoon dark soy sauce
pinch of fine sea salt
pinch of ground white pepper
1 teaspoon sesame oil
250 g (9 oz/generous 1⅓ cups) cooked basmati rice (or 1 microwavable pouch)

FOR THE DRESSING

1 tablespoon light soy sauce
1 tablespoon rice vinegar
½ tablespoon honey

TOPPINGS

toasted sesame seeds
veggies of your choice, such as julienned carrots, shredded spinach, broccoli florets, shredded cabbage, green beans or beansprouts
boiled eggs
pickled vegetables
chilli oil

METHOD

1. Combine the salmon chunks, honey, soy sauce, salt, white pepper and sesame oil in a bowl.
2. Preheat the oven to 160°C fan (180°C/350°F/Gas 4), place the salmon pieces on a lined baking tray (pan) and cook for 12–15 minutes until cooked through. Alternatively, you can use an air fryer at 180°C (350°F) for about 10 minutes.
3. Meanwhile, prepare any toppings you would like to add to your rice bowl. If using vegetables like broccoli, cabbage, green beans or beansprouts, blanch these in boiling water until tender, then drain.
4. To make the dressing, mix together the light soy sauce, rice vinegar and honey in a bowl.
5. Build your rice bowl by dividing the hot rice between bowls, then adding the salmon and any other toppings you would like. Finally, drizzle with the dressing before serving.

Pan-fried Sea Bass with Ginger and Spring Onions

Mum used to cook us a lot of sea bass. Whether it was the whole fish or just fillets, she made sure we ate seafood at least once a week and it usually coincided with the Tuesday market in Lisburn, Northern Ireland, where she bought her fish weekly.

This is a simple recipe that utilizes store-cupboard ingredients, including ginger, spring onions (scallions) and soy sauce. You can change up the fish or even use a whole fish, but note that it will take longer to pan-fry. Enjoy with rice, noodles, salad or stir-fried vegetables.

Serves 4
Prep: 5 minutes
Cook: 15 minutes

INGREDIENTS

4 sea bass fillets, patted dry with paper towels
1 tablespoon vegetable oil
1 thumb-size piece of fresh ginger root, sliced into thin matchsticks
2 spring onions (scallions), finely sliced on the diagonal
1 red chilli, deseeded and finely sliced
1 tablespoon light soy sauce

METHOD

1. First, score the skin of the fish four times on each fillet (this stops the skin tightening and curling).
2. Heat the vegetable oil in a frying pan over a medium heat. Place the fish in the pan, skin side facing down, and fry for 3–5 minutes until the skin is crispy, then flip and cook for 2 minutes on the other side.
3. Using a fish slice, lift the fish fillets out onto a plate, skin side up.
4. In the same pan, fry the ginger and spring onions for about 1 minute until fragrant (if you want the dish really spicy, add the chilli now, otherwise wait until the end).
5. Scatter the spring onions and ginger over the fish fillets and drizzle with the soy sauce, then sprinkle over the chilli.

Seafood Udon Noodles

This recipe came about after I was sent a bag of frozen seafood as a replacement for frozen king prawns (jumbo shrimp) in my online shop. Determined to make the recipe work, I just treated it exactly the same as I would a prawn version of this dish and it was a triumph.

Serves 2
Prep: 5 minutes
Cook: 15 minutes

INGREDIENTS

300 g (10½ oz) packet of mixed cooked, frozen seafood
1 tablespoon vegetable oil
1 teaspoon finely chopped garlic
1 small onion, grated
1 carrot, peeled and grated
½ courgette (zucchini), grated
1 heaped tablespoon oyster sauce
2 packets (approximately 300 g/10½ oz) of ready-to-use udon noodles
2 tablespoons water
1 teaspoon light soy sauce
1 teaspoon sesame oil
pinch of ground white pepper

METHOD

1. Bring a saucepan of water to the boil, then add the mixed frozen seafood and blanch for 1 minute. Drain immediately and plunge into cold water to stop the seafood from cooking any further.
2. Heat the vegetable oil in a wok over a high heat and fry the garlic for 30–60 seconds until fragrant. Add the onion, carrot and courgette and reduce the heat to medium. Cook for 3–4 minutes until the vegetables are soft, stirring constantly.
3. Add the oyster sauce and stir through, then place the noodles in the middle of the wok, add the water and cover with a lid. After a couple of minutes, remove the lid and carefully stir the noodles into the other ingredients. The noodles should have started to soften and separate. If not, just place the lid back on for another minute or so.
4. Add the soy sauce, sesame oil and white pepper and give everything a good stir until well combined.
5. Finally, add the seafood and stir until it has heated through and is evenly distributed through the noodles. You're ready to serve!

Stuffed Steamed Tofu

This is another dish from my memories . . . My mum used to make this recipe using firm tofu (bean curd) and a pork and prawn (shrimp) mixture. I have adjusted the filling to include prawns, ginger, carrot and spring onion (scallion), for a different flavour profile. I have also gone with silken tofu, as I prefer the softer texture, but if you can't get hold of it, then just use firm tofu.

Serves 4
Prep: 5 minutes
Cook: 15 minutes

INGREDIENTS

350 g (12 oz) block of firm, medium or silken tofu (bean curd)
1 large spring onion (scallion), white parts roughly chopped and green parts finely chopped
¼ teaspoon chicken stock powder
½ teaspoon grated fresh ginger root
¼ carrot, peeled and roughly chopped
½ teaspoon sesame oil
½ teaspoon fine sea salt
good pinch of ground white pepper
1 teaspoon cornflour (cornstarch)
100 g (3½ oz) raw peeled prawns (shrimp), roughly chopped
2 tablespoons light soy sauce

METHOD

1. Place the block of tofu on a heatproof dish, then slice it widthways into pieces on a chopping board. I sliced mine into four pieces, but you could also make eight smaller pieces by cutting them in half.
2. Using a small, sharp knife, carefully cut a 3 mm (⅛ in) border around each block of tofu, being careful not to slice all the way down. Using a teaspoon, carefully spoon out the middle of the tofu and set it aside. These holes are where the prawn mixture will go. This is slightly fiddly but worth it.
3. Put the spooned-out tofu into a food processor along with the white parts of the spring onion, the chicken stock powder, ginger, carrot, sesame oil, salt, white pepper and cornflour. Blend until smooth. Now add the prawns and pulse to your desired texture. You may like to have chunks of prawn in the mixture or you might prefer more of a purée.
4. Divide the prawn mixture evenly between the holes in the tofu blocks and gently smooth down the top.
5. Prepare a steamer, then place the dish with the tofu blocks inside the piping-hot steamer and steam for 10–12 minutes until the prawn mixture is cooked. Remove from the steamer and drizzle over the soy sauce, then top with the spring onion greens (I like to use scissors to snip the spring onions directly over the tofu as I find this easiest).

Beef and Courgette Stir-fry

I love packing our family meals with vegetables, so courgettes (zucchini) are always part of my weekly shop. Back at the start of my journey as a mum, they were one of the vegetables I used regularly in recipes for weaning because they become so soft when cooked. As the kids got older, I moved on to grating them into their meals. Now, I leave the courgettes chunky in dishes.

Serves 2
Prep: 5–10 minutes
Cook: 10 minutes

INGREDIENTS

250 g (9 oz) rump (sirloin) steak, finely sliced against the grain
1 teaspoon Shaoxing wine
1 teaspoon light soy sauce
1 heaped teaspoon cornflour (cornstarch)
2 pinches of ground white pepper
1 teaspoon sesame oil
1 tablespoon vegetable oil
1 garlic clove, finely chopped
1 small courgette (zucchini), sliced into 5-mm (¼-in) thick half-moons
1 heaped tablespoon oyster sauce
pinch of fine sea salt
basmati rice or noodles, to serve

METHOD

1. Combine the sliced steak, Shaoxing wine, soy sauce, cornflour, a pinch of white pepper and sesame oil in a bowl and mix well.
2. Heat a wok over a high heat, then add the sesame oil and flash-fry the steak pieces for a couple of minutes on each side. Transfer the steak to a dish. Do not clean the wok.
3. Add the vegetable oil to the wok along with the garlic and fry for a minute or so until fragrant, then add the courgette and spread out in an even layer. Fry for 1 minute to brown the courgette a little on one side, then flip over and cook for a further minute.
4. Now add the oyster sauce, salt and another pinch of pepper and give everything a good mix. Finally, add the beef strips again and cook for a further 1–2 minutes until everything is well combined and coated. Taste and adjust the seasoning if needed.
5. Serve with some steaming hot basmati rice or noodles.

Pork and Chilli Bean Stir-fry with Spinach

I love to throw together a recipe just based on what I have in my refrigerator, freezer, larder and cupboards. Spinach is always in my refrigerator and one time when I had bought minced (ground) pork to make dumplings, I realized I didn't have any wrappers – so this recipe was born!

Serves 2
Prep: 5 minutes
Cook: 15 minutes

INGREDIENTS

250 g (9 oz) minced (ground) pork
1 teaspoon cornflour (cornstarch)
1 teaspoon light soy sauce
1 teaspoon sesame oil
1 teaspoon vegetable oil
1 teaspoon finely chopped or grated garlic
1 teaspoon finely chopped or grated fresh ginger root
2–3 tablespoons *toban djan* (fermented chilli bean paste), depending on how spicy you like it
200 g (7 oz) Chinese spinach or spinach, roughly chopped

METHOD

1. Combine the pork, cornflour, soy sauce and sesame oil in a bowl and mix well. Leave for at least 5 minutes to marinate.
2. Heat the vegetable oil in a wok over a high heat and fry the garlic and ginger for about 1 minute, just until fragrant. Watch the garlic and ginger don't burn. If they do start to catch, add a splash of water.
3. Add the marinated pork and break up with a wooden spoon, then cook for 2–3 minutes.
4. Add the *toban djan* and cook for about 5 minutes.
5. Finally, add the Chinese spinach or spinach and cook for a further 2–3 minutes. Serve.

Pork and Preserved Vegetables

This is another childhood classic that Mum used to make on repeat. The lovely contrast between the soft meat and the texture and flavour of the preserved vegetables is delicious. Mum always used a brown, bulbous-looking jar of Tianjin preserved vegetables. In Cantonese, these vegetables are called *dong choi*, which literally translates as 'winter vegetable'. Tianjin preserved vegetables are a salty condiment that can be used to flavour so many dishes and are great for dumpling fillings or as a salty garnish. There are so many varieties of preserved vegetables, so you do not have to go with the Tianjin brand I use.

Serves 2
Prep: 5 minutes
Cook: 15 minutes

INGREDIENTS

2 tablespoons preserved vegetables, finely chopped
250 g (9 oz) minced (ground) pork
1 teaspoon sesame oil
1 teaspoon light soy sauce
1 teaspoon Shaoxing wine
1 heaped teaspoon cornflour
large pinch of ground white pepper
rice, to serve

METHOD:

1. Add the preserved vegetables to a small heatproof bowl and just cover with boiling water. Leave to soak for about 5 minutes (this is to remove the excess salt), then rinse in cold water and drain.
2. Now combine the rinsed preserved vegetables with the pork, sesame oil, soy sauce, Shaoxing wine, cornflour and white pepper in a bowl and mix to combine.
3. Put this mixture in a heatproof dish and press it down flat to create a large, round patty.
4. Prepare a steamer, then place the dish in the steamer and steam for about 15 minutes until the pork is just cooked through.
5. Serve hot with rice. The cooking liquid from the meat patty also tastes delicious spooned over the hot rice.

Mum's Steamed Milk Egg Pudding

Mum used to make these as a quick dessert. They are call *dun dan*, aka 'steamed eggs'. I loved these smooth and soothing desserts when I was little. I find them so comforting to eat.

Serves 4
Prep: 5 minutes
Cook: 15 minutes

INGREDIENTS

75 ml (2½ fl oz/5 tablespoons) water
50 g (1¾ oz/scant ¼ cup) caster (superfine) sugar
250 ml (8 fl oz/1 cup) whole milk
3 large (US extra large) eggs, beaten
1 teaspoon vanilla extract

METHOD

1. Heat the water and sugar in a small saucepan over a low heat until the sugar has dissolved, then remove from the heat.
2. Whisk the milk and eggs into the sugar water until well combined.
3. Pour the mixture through a sieve (strainer) into four small heatproof bowls, then cover each bowl tightly with some cling film (plastic wrap).
4. Prepare a steamer, heating to a high heat until it is fully steaming. Place the bowls in the steamer and steam the puddings for 10 minutes. Check the puddings at 10 minutes – you want the middle to be quite jiggly and the sides just set. If they are too wobbly, keep steaming for a couple more minutes.
5. Remove the puddings from the steamer and peel away the cling flim carefully. Leave to set for a further 5 minutes before enjoying.

Ginger Pudding

This is a really popular dessert in Hong Kong – the literal translation of the name in Chinese is 'ginger juice pudding milk'. The recipe consists of only three ingredients and there's no baking or steaming required because the fresh ginger juice helps to set the heated whole milk.

Serves 1
Prep: 15 minutes
Cook: 5 minutes

INGREDIENTS

175 ml (6 fl oz/¾ cup) whole milk
2 heaped teaspoons caster (superfine) sugar
30 g (1 oz) fresh ginger root, peeled

METHOD

1. Combine the milk and sugar in a small saucepan over a low heat and heat until there are bubbles forming around the edges. If a skin forms, remove it with a fork.
2. Grate the ginger into a sieve (strainer) placed over a bowl. Then, using a spoon, push and squeeze the juice out of the ginger through the sieve. You need between 2 teaspoons and 1 tablespoon of ginger juice – approximately 10–15 ml.
3. Remove the milk from the heat and swirl it around in the pan to evenly distribute the heat. If the milk has boiled over, leave it to rest and cool for a couple of minutes before swirling in the pan.
4. Now pour the milk quickly over the ginger juice, then leave to set for 10 minutes. Serve.

30 MINUTES OR LESS

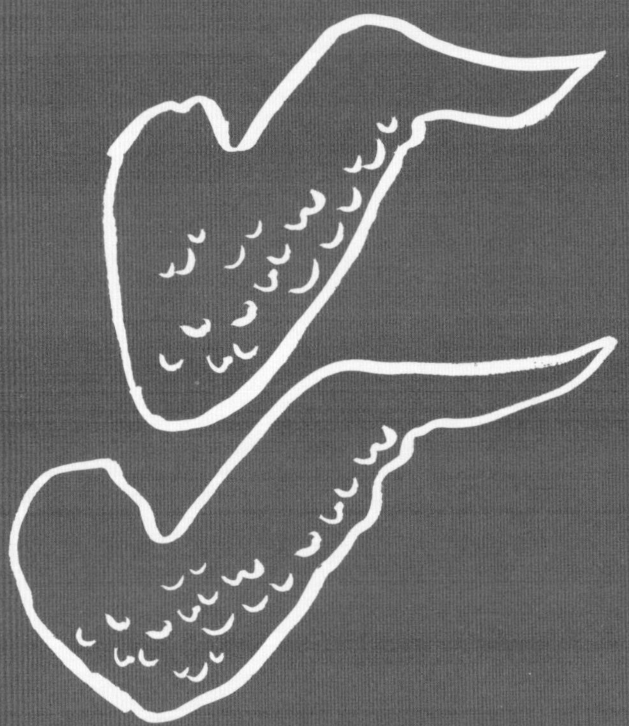

The world is your oyster if you have 30 minutes to spare! This chapter is the biggest and most diverse in terms of flavour and types of dishes, including takeaway favourites like the iconic Irish King Prawn Spice Bag (page 138), which is packed with salted chilli chips (fries), veg and – instead of the usual chicken – king prawns (jumbo shrimp).

CHAPTER FOUR

Tomato Egg Drop Soup

This is a quick, heart-warming soup. I grew up eating soup daily – it was one of the dishes that was a must with our dinner! My mum was so traditional in the way she fed us; soup was part and parcel of all our meals.

Serves 2
Prep: 5 minutes
Cook: 20 minutes

INGREDIENTS

1 teaspoon vegetable oil
2 large spring onions (scallions), white and green parts separated and cut into 5 cm (2 in) pieces
10 g (½ oz) fresh ginger root, sliced into two thick pieces
3 large tomatoes (about 300 g /10½ oz), sliced into wedges
1 litre (34 fl oz/4¼ cups) water
1 teaspoon vegetable or chicken stock powder or 1 stock cube, crumbled
1 large (US extra large) egg, beaten
fine sea salt and ground white pepper

METHOD

1. Heat the oil in a saucepan over a high heat and then fry the white parts of the spring onion and the ginger for 2 minutes until fragrant.
2. Add the tomatoes and cook for 1 minute, stirring constantly.
3. Pour in the water, then add the stock powder or cube.
4. Bring to the boil, then simmer for 10–15 minutes until the broth has reduced down and the flavours become more concentrated.
5. Lower the heat and then drizzle in the beaten egg. Depending on how you drizzle in the egg, it will cook in chunks or ribbons.
6. Taste and season with salt and white pepper, then serve topped with a sprinkling of spring onion greens.

My Mum's Special Porridge

My mum used to make this for us at least two or three times a week for breakfast before school. The addition of egg and condensed milk is influenced by her childhood in Hong Kong. It definitely kept me full, and it was great after doing my morning swimming session with the swim club.

Serves 2
Prep: 10 minutes
Cook: 15 minutes

INGREDIENTS

80 g (2¾ oz/¾ cup) rolled oats
500 ml (17 fl oz/generous 2 cups) cold water, or as needed
2 tablespoons condensed milk, or to taste
2 small eggs, beaten

TOPPING SUGGESTIONS

fresh fruit, such as blackberries and raspberries
fruit compote
jam (jelly)
honey
nuts and seeds
yoghurt

METHOD

1. Put the oats, water and condensed milk in a saucepan, bring to the boil, then reduce to a simmer and cook for about 10 minutes until the porridge has reached your desired consistency. I like it quite thick, but add a splash of milk or water if you prefer a thinner porridge.
2. Remove the pan from the heat and quickly beat in the eggs. Keep beating, so the eggs don't scramble. (You might see small flecks of the egg in the porridge but you don't taste these –they just give the porridge a really rich and luxurious flavour).
3. I like to top my porridge with berries, mixed seeds and more condensed milk! It is delicious!

'Swiss' Chicken Wings

These are very tasty, fragrant wings that are not actually from Switzerland. The story goes that a foreigner in Hong Kong was served these wings and the waiter mispronounced 'sweet' as 'Swiss'. The name stuck and the dish on the menu was changed to 'Swiss' chicken wings.

There will be quite a lot of sauce left over, so do not waste this – use it to marinate or cook other meats. I often use it to make a quick fried rice, as it has so much flavour that I don't need to add anything extra to jazz it up.

Serves 4
Prep: 5 minutes
Cook: 25 minutes

INGREDIENTS

1 kg (2 lb 4 oz) chicken wings
50 g (1¾ oz) fresh ginger root, sliced
3 large spring onions (scallions), cut into chunks
4 tablespoons oyster sauce
100 ml (3½ fl oz/scant ½ cup) light soy sauce
25 ml (1½ tablespoons) dark soy sauce
3 star anise
1 cinnamon stick
8 tablespoons soft brown sugar (light or dark)
1 litre (34 fl oz/4¼ cups) water

METHOD

1. Put the wings in a large saucepan and cover with water. Bring to the boil and cook for 5 minutes, skimming any scum off the top. Drain, then set the wings aside.
2. Combine all the remaining ingredients in the same pan, mix well and put over a high heat.
3. Return the wings to the pan and once everything is bubbling, reduce the heat and simmer for 20–25 minutes, turning the wings every 5 minutes to make sure they are submerged and cooked through.
4. Serve as a starter, snack or as part of a meal.
5. These wings can also be made in advance. Follow steps 1–3, then leave the wings in the saucepan until cool. Once coooled, transfer the wings to a large bowl and cover with tin foil or cling film (plastic wrap) and refrigerate until ready to eat. To reheat, place in a saucepan over a high heat until the sauce is boiling and the wings are heated through.

Chinese Rice Cake and *Lap Cheong* Stir-fry

I think rice cakes are very underrated, so I have used them in a few recipes in this book. They add so much texture to a dish, and I love the contrast they give. They are also like sponges and can absorb flavour very well. This stir-fry was thrown together from bits and bobs I had in my kitchen, but I have ensured you can make it even more quickly by using fresh shiitake mushrooms. So tasty! This, for me, is the perfect stir-fry meal - quick and packed with protein from the *lap cheong* (Chinese cured sausage) and veggies, plus those all-important carbs from the rice cakes. If you have extra time, you can also use dried shiitake mushrooms in this recipe - just soak them in hot water for 20 minutes and then follow the recipe as below.

Serves 2
Prep: 10 minutes
Cook: 15 minutes

INGREDIENTS

1 teaspoon vegetable oil
2 *lap cheong* (Chinese cured sausages), soaked in boiling water for 2 minutes, then skin removed and sliced on the diagonal
1 teaspoon finely chopped fresh ginger root
1 heaped teaspoon finely chopped garlic
1 tablespoon dark soy sauce
1 heaped teaspoon caster (superfine) sugar
large pinch of ground white pepper
2 tablespoons Shaoxing wine
2 tablespoons oyster sauce
250 g (9 oz) ready-to-cook ambient rice cakes (they should be firm to the touch but not dried)
120 g (4 oz) shiitake mushrooms, roughly chopped
200 g (7 oz) pak choi (bok choy), quartered lengthways if large, halved if smaller
1 teaspoon sesame oil

METHOD

1. Heat the vegetable oil in a wok over a high heat and fry the sliced *lap cheong* until lightly browned, which will take about 2 minutes. Remove the *lap cheong* and set aside. Do not clean the wok.
2. Add the ginger and garlic and cook for about 1 minute until fragrant, then add the soy sauce, sugar, white pepper, Shaoxing wine and oyster sauce. Simmer for a couple of minutes.
3. Add the rice cakes and mushrooms and cook for another 5–8 minutes until the rice cakes soften. They will have the texture of firm jelly. Add a splash of water if the rice cakes start to stick to the bottom of the wok.
4. Now add the pak choi and cook for another couple of minutes until it is just cooked. Drizzle the sesame oil around the edge of the wok and toss through.
5. I eat this stir-fry as it is but you could also serve it with steamed rice.

Quick Dumplings

My children are addicted to dumplings in all their forms, and this is the quickest way I know to make them. Using a food processor to blend the ingredients helps to speed things up. You can make either gyozas or wontons, and boiling them is much quicker than frying or deep-frying, but you can also pop them in an air fryer.

Makes 16–20 dumplings
Prep: 10 minutes
Cook: up to 15 minutes

INGREDIENTS

150 g (5½ oz) chicken breast (about 1 breast)
50 g (1¾ oz) mushrooms (white, chestnut/cremini or shiitake)
1 spring onion (scallion), roughly chopped
1 heaped teaspoon cornflour (cornstarch), plus extra for dusting if you are frying he dumplings
1 teaspoon sesame oil
½ teaspoon garlic powder
1 teaspoon dark soy sauce
¼ teaspoon fine sea salt
good pinch of ground white pepper
16–20 gyoza or wonton wrappers
1 tablespoon vegetable oil (optional, if frying)
dipping sauce of your choice, to serve (optional)

METHOD

1. Put all the ingredients except the wrappers (and the vegetable oil and dipping sauce) in a food processor and blend for about 1 minute until a rough paste forms.
2. To make the dumplings, spoon about a teaspoon of filling into the middle of each wrapper, then dab water around the edge of the wrapper. Fold the wrapper around the filling in whatever shape you would like (just make sure the filling is sealed in well). I just gather all the edges and pinch them together in the middle to make an easy wonton.
3. To fry gyozas, dust the bottom of each one with cornflour. Heat 1 tablespoon of oil in a frying pan over a medium heat and fry the dumplings on one side for 2–3 minutes until lightly golden on the bottom.
4. Add 100 ml (3½ fl oz/scant ½ cup) water, cover and steam-cook for 8–10 minutes until the water evaporates and the gyozas are cooked through.
5. To boil gyozas or wontons, half-fill a saucepan with water and bring to the boil. Drop in the gyozas or wontons and boil for 3–5 minutes until cooked through.
6. To deep-fry wontons, pour vegetable oil into a small, heavy-duty saucepan over a high heat to a depth of 5 cm (2 in). Test if the oil is ready by lowering the handle of a wooden spoon into it. If bubbles fizz around the handle, you are ready to deep-fry.
7. Carefully lower 5–6 wontons into the pan at a time. Once they float to the top and are golden, they are ready. Take the wontons out of the pan and drain on some paper towel.
8. Eat the dumplings as they are or with a dipping sauce of your choice, such as soy sauce, black vinegar or chilli crisp oil.

Spring Onion Pancakes

In Northern Ireland, we also call spring onions scallions – they're such a fab ingredient that add so much flavour to dishes. This is a super-quick version of the classic scallion pancake (that normally takes about an hour to make). I have used cornflour (cornstarch) as well as plain (all-purpose) flour for a flaky texture and even more flavour. The white parts of the spring onions are used to flavour the oil.

Serves 2
Prep: 15 min
Cook: 15 min

INGREDIENTS

100 g (3½ oz/generous ¾ cup) plain (all-purpose) flour
2 tablespoons cornflour (cornstarch)
½ teaspoon fine sea salt
large pinch of ground white pepper
75 ml (2½ fl oz/5 tablespoons) boiling water
1 teaspoon sesame oil
3 spring onions (scallions), white parts halved and green parts finely chopped
vegetable oil, for frying and rolling

TO SERVE

chilli crisp oil (or chilli crisp and mayo or yoghurt!)

METHOD

1. Combine the flour, cornflour, salt and white pepper in a bowl. Using a wooden spoon, keep stirring the flour mixture while you pour the boiling water into the bowl. Mix to a rough dough, then add the sesame oil and mix through.
2. Cover the bowl with a plate and leave to rest at room temperature for 15 minutes.
3. While the dough is resting, pour about 4 tablespoons of vegetable oil into a large frying pan and add the white parts of the spring onions. Heat for a couple of minutes over a high heat until the spring onions have turned brown but are not burned, then remove the pan from the heat and set aside. Leave the spring onions in the oil while you continue preparing the dough.
4. On a lightly oiled surface, knead the dough for a few minutes, then roll it out into a rectangle about 2 mm (⅛ in) thick. Sprinkle the spring onion greens evenly all over the dough.
5. Starting from one of the long edges, tightly roll up the dough into a sausage. Cut the sausage into four pieces, then roll each piece into a longer sausage.
6. Curl each sausage into a tight, round spiral and then flatten on the work surface with the palm of your hand. Using a lightly oiled rolling pin, roll the spirals out into circles about 2–3 mm (⅛ in) thick.
7. Remove the spring onions from the infused oil, then heat the oil in the pan over a high heat. Fry the spring onion pancakes for a couple of minutes on each side until browned. If all four pancakes won't fit into the pan, decant half the oil for the next batch. Serve with mayo, yoghurt and chilli crisp oil.

Crispy Tofu with Black Bean Sauce

This crispy tofu (bean curd) is so easy to prepare – you can even use an air fryer to get it nice and crunchy. It's so delicious topped with black bean sauce.

Serves 2
Prep: 5 minutes
Cook: 20–25 minutes

INGREDIENTS

250 g (9 oz) firm tofu (bean curd)
1 heaped tablespoon cornflour (cornstarch)
1 tablespoon vegetable oil or a couple of pumps of oil spray
½ x quantity Black Bean Sauce (page 122)
fine sea salt and ground white pepper
finely sliced spring onions (scallions), to serve

METHOD

1. Preheat the oven to 160°C fan (180°C/350°F/Gas 4) or an air fryer to 200°C (400°F).
2. Chop the tofu into roughly 16 cubes, then lay them out on paper towels. Press with more paper towels on top to absorb any excess liquid in the tofu. You want the tofu to be as dry as possible so that it crisps up.
3. Sprinkle salt and white pepper over the tofu cubes, then dust them all over with the cornflour.
4. Drizzle or brush the tofu with the oil or spray it with some oil spray, then cook in the oven on a baking tray (pan) for about 20 minutes or in the air fryer for 12–15 minutes. Toss the cubes halfway through the cooking and spray them with a little bit more oil if they are looking too dry.
5. Once cooked, place the crispy tofu on a plate, drizzle over the warm black bean sauce and garnish with spring onions to serve.

Veggie Mince Lettuce Wraps

These lettuce wraps (called *san choi bao* in Chinese) can be made with any type of minced (ground) meat or soy mince (TVP), which I have used here. The soy mince soaks up all the different seasonings and can be cooked from frozen in minutes, which is a real time-saver. This dish is packed with flavour and is great for sharing. If you decide to use minced meat, there may be some extra liquid when cooking, in which case, add a little cornflour (cornstarch) paste (see page 17) towards the end of cooking.

Serves 4
Prep: 5 minutes
Cook: 20 minutes

INGREDIENTS

1 tablespoon vegetable oil
1 tablespoon finely chopped or grated garlic
1 tablespoon finely chopped or grated fresh ginger root
1 onion, finely diced
1 celery stalk, finely diced
1 carrot, peeled and finely diced
handful of mushrooms of your choice, finely diced
300 g (10½ oz) frozen soy mince (TVP) or minced (ground) meat (chicken, beef, pork or turkey)
2 tablespoons light soy sauce
1 tablespoon dark soy sauce
1 tablespoon vegetarian oyster sauce (or regular oyster sauce)
1 tablespoon Shaoxing wine
1 teaspoon sesame oil
fine sea salt and ground white pepper

TO SERVE

sliced chillies
sliced spring onions (scallions)
1 large gem lettuce or small iceberg lettuce, leaves separated

METHOD

1. Heat the vegetable oil in a wok or frying pan over a high heat and fry the garlic and ginger for about 2 minutes until fragrant.
2. Add the onion, celery, carrot and mushrooms and cook for about 10 minutes until softened.
3. Add the soy mince (or your meat of choice) and cook for about 2 minutes.
4. Now add the light and dark soy sauces, oyster sauce, Shaoxing wine and sesame oil and cook for a further 5 minutes. Taste and adjust the seasoning with salt and white pepper.
5. Serve garnished with chillies and spring onions, piled into lettuce leaves.

Tofu Dan Dan-style Noodles

Dan dan noodles originated from Sichuan, China, and were sold by street vendors carrying them on bamboo poles. 'Dan dan' references how the noodles are carried on these poles. While usually made with pork, this crumbled tofu (bean curd) version of dan dan noodles is so tasty and packed with flavour. I decided to try it out with spaghetti, which is a frequently used ingredient in Hong Kong, and it was a great success.

Serves 2
Prep: 5 minutes
Cook: 20–25 minutes

INGREDIENTS

100 g (3½ oz) spaghetti
1 tablespoon vegetable oil
1 teaspoon finely chopped garlic
½ teaspoon Chinese five-spice powder
½ tablespoon chilli oil
1 teaspoon hoisin sauce
1 teaspoon Shaoxing wine
2 teaspoons dark soy sauce
1 teaspoon sesame oil
1 tablespoon tahini
1 teaspoon sugar
good pinch of fine sea salt and ground white pepper
200–250 g (7–9 oz) medium or firm tofu (bean curd), crumbled

TO SERVE

toasted peanuts
sliced spring onions (scallions)

METHOD

1. Bring a saucepan of water to the boil and cook the spaghetti according to the package instructions until al dente, then drain, reserving a cup of the pasta cooking water.
2. Meanwhile, heat the vegetable oil in a wok or frying pan over a high heat and fry the garlic and Chinese five-spice powder for 30–60 seconds until fragrant.
3. Add the hoisin sauce, Shaoxing wine, dark soy sauce, sesame oil, tahini, sugar, salt and white pepper, and simmer for a couple of minutes.
4. Add the tofu and break it up further with a wooden spoon. Add a ladle of pasta water and simmer for 3–5 minutes, then taste and adjust the seasoning as needed.
5. Add the hot spaghetti and toss through the sauce until the spaghetti is fully coated.
6. Garnish with the peanuts and spring onions.

How to Make Silver Pin Noodles

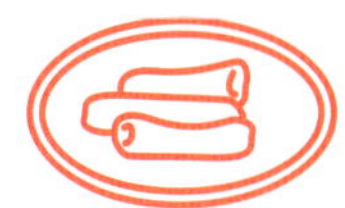

These noodles are traditionally a Hakka dish (which is my dad's heritage), made by the Hakka people from rice flour. I remember them being served in a very simple broth made with chicken stock, ginger, garlic and spring onions (scallions), which takes just minutes to make. Or use them in the Duck and Silver Pin Noodle Soup (see page 58).

Serves 1
Prep: 20 minutes
Cook: 5 minutes

INGREDIENTS

75 g (2½ oz/scant ⅔ cup) wheat starch
25 g (1 oz/3 tablespoons) rice flour
1½ teaspoons vegetable oil, plus extra for tossing the noodles
100 ml (3½ fl oz/scant ½ cup) boiling water
fine sea salt

TIP

I have made enough for one person in this recipe, but the ingredients can easily be multiplied for the number of people who want to eat these delicious noodles. You can also batch-cook the noodles and, once cool, store them in the refrigerator in an airtight container for up to four days or in the freezer for up to a month.

METHOD

1. Combine the wheat starch, rice flour, half teaspoon of the oil and a pinch of salt in a bowl. Using chopsticks, keep stirring the flour mixture while you pour the boiling water into the bowl. This will take about 3 minutes to fully combine and the mixture will become very thick. At this stage, knead the dough with your hands (wear a pair of rubber gloves if it is too hot) in the bowl until it comes together into a smooth ball with no cracks. If it is too dry, add a little bit of water; if too wet, add a little bit more wheat starch.
2. Divide the dough into two equal pieces, then roll each one into logs. Keep one wrapped in cling film (plastic wrap), so it doesn't dry out while you are working with the other log of dough. Divide the first log into tiny pieces – each piece should be about the size of a small marble and weigh no more that 2–3 g (⅛ oz). You can make the pieces whatever size you like, but this will affect the cooking time.
3. Next, roll each piece between your palms with your hands slightly cupped until they form a long shape with tapered ends, like a needle. Repeat until all the dough is used up. This took me 20 minutes, but the more times you do it, the quicker you will get.
4. Bring a large saucepan of water to a vigorous boil, then add a good pinch of salt along with the remaining teaspoon of oil. Carefully and gradually drop the noodles into the water, stirring constantly, so that they don't sink to the bottom or stick together. Keep stirring. Once the noodles float to the top, use a slotted spoon to remove them and immediately rinse under cold water. Toss the noodles in a little oil, so they don't stick together. Use straight away or store in an airtight container in the refrigerator for up to four days.

Black Bean Sauce

My mum used to make a huge variety of dishes with black beans: steamed fish or tofu (bean curd) with black beans; chicken, beef, pork or prawns (shrimp) with black bean sauce; stuffed and fried tofu with black bean sauce; a variety of shellfish with black beans. A container of *dou see* (fermented Chinese black beans) lives in my refrigerator, ready to use at any moment. However, do not get these confused with the black beans native to the Americas. Chinese black beans are actually fermented salted black soya beans. There are hundreds of varieties of soya bean in many different colours. Young green soya beans are also known as edamame beans. More mature soya beans, which are used to make soya milk and tofu. Soy sauce is made from cooked soya beans combined with wheat, salt and a fermenting agent. Soya beans are rich in protein, fibre, vitamins and minerals and are a truly versatile ingredient with many by-products. Chinese black beans can be bought in your local Chinese supermarket or online – they can be found dried in a packet or rehydrated in a tin.

Makes about 500 ml (17 fl oz/ generous 2 cups)
Prep: 15 minutes
Cook: 15 minutes

INGREDIENTS

2 tablespoons (about 25 g/1 oz) dried fermented black beans
2 tablespoons vegetable, sunflower or rapeseed (canola) oil
½ tablespoon finely chopped fresh ginger root
1 large garlic clove, finely chopped
1 tablespoon Shaoxing wine
1 tablespoon light soy sauce
large pinch of caster (superfine) sugar
½ teaspoon vegetable stock powder or ½ vegetable stock cube, crumbled
1 teaspoon sesame oil
400 ml (14 fl oz/generous 1½ cups) water
1 tablespoon cornflour (cornstarch) mixed with 2 tablespoons water to make a paste
fine sea salt and a pinch of ground white pepper

TIP

This sauce will keep in an airtight container in the refrigerator for up to five days or in the freezer for up to a month.

METHOD

1. The fermented black beans come in a small plastic bag, so remove any pieces of dried ginger or other ingredients first. Then, put the beans in a heatproof bowl and cover with boiling water, and leave to soak for at least 15 minutes. Once soaked, drain and set aside.
2. Heat the vegetable, sunflower or rapeseed oil in a wok or saucepan over a high heat and fry the ginger and garlic for 2 minutes until fragrant, stirring constantly to make sure they don't burn.
3. Add the black beans and cook for another minute, then add the Shaoxing wine and cook for a minute more.
4. Add the soy sauce, sugar, stock powder or cube, sesame oil and white pepper. Taste and adjust the seasoning as needed.
5. Pour in the water and simmer gently for about 10 minutes. The longer you cook the beans, the softer they become, eventually starting to disintegrate into the sauce. This is all dependent on your texture preference. If you like beans softer, add a bit more water, so you can cook the sauce for longer.
6. Remove the pan from the heat and mix in the cornflour paste. Keep stirring as you bring the sauce to the boil. The sauce will thicken and become glossy.
7. Taste the sauce again. If you think it is too intense, add more water. If you want it thicker, add more cornflour paste a teaspoon at a time and bring to the boil again.

Hokkien Fried Rice

I spoke to my dad about this dish and he told me that it was created to use up bits and bobs hanging around the kitchen. It is a fried rice dish with a thick 'gravy' containing lots of different ingredients poured over the top. It is so tasty and something I always order for my family when we are out! It literally has everything you want in one dish.

Serves 4
Prep: 10 minutes
Cook: 15 minutes

INGREDIENTS

1 carrot (about 100 g/3½ oz), peeled and diced
100 g (3½ oz) tenderstem broccoli (broccolini), chopped into small pieces
1 tablespoon vegetable oil, plus extra as needed
4 medium (US large) eggs, beaten
500 g (1 lb 2 oz/scant 3 cups) cooked and cooled basmati rice (or 2 microwavable pouches)
½ tablespoon dark soy sauce
1 teaspoon sesame oil, plus extra for drizzling
2 tablespoons light soy sauce
2 tablespoons oyster sauce
2 tablespoons Shaoxing wine
1 teaspoon chicken stock powder or 1 chicken stock cube, crumbled
150 g (5½ oz) cooked or raw peeled king prawns (jumbo shrimp), chopped
200 g (7 oz) cooked chicken or duck, chopped
2 handfuls of mushrooms of your choice, such as chestnut (cremini), button (white) or shiitake, chopped into cubes
250 ml (8 fl oz/1 cup) water
1 tablespoon cornflour (cornstarch) paste (see page 17)
fine sea salt and ground white pepper

METHOD

1. Put the carrot and broccoli in a saucepan over a high heat with a large splash of water, cover and cook for 1 minute. Drain and set aside on a plate.
2. Heat the vegetable oil in a wok over a high heat and add the eggs. Cook for about 2 minutes, swirling the pan every 15 seconds, so the egg fills the gaps to create a lightly cooked omelette. Transfer the omelette to a plate.
3. Add another drizzle of vegetable oil to the wok, add the rice and use a wooden spoon to break up any lumps.
4. Now add the dark soy sauce and toss it through the rice. Drizzle the sesame oil around the edge of the rice, then mix through.
5. Add the omelette to the wok and use your spoon to break down the egg into smaller pieces, then evenly distribute it through the rice. Add a pinch of salt and white pepper. Pour the rice into a large serving dish.
6. Pour the light soy sauce, oyster sauce and Shaoxing wine into the wok along with the chicken stock powder or cube and cook for a couple of minutes.
7. Add the prawns, chicken or duck, and your choice of mushrooms and cook for a further 2 minutes.
8. Reduce the heat and add the water and cornflour paste, then increase the heat to high and cook until the sauce thickens. Add the carrots and broccoli and stir through, just to heat through the vegetables.
9. Pour the sauce over the rice and serve.

Baked Pork Chop Rice

This is such a classic Hong Kong dish. It can be found in all the *cha chaan teng* cafés, which serve a fusion of Western and Eastern cuisine. Here, a juicy pork chop is laid over rice and topped with tomato sauce and melted cheese. Don't knock it until you've tried it.

Serves 2
Prep: 10 minutes
Cook: 20 minutes

INGREDIENTS

2 boneless pork chops
1 heaped teaspoon cornflour (cornstarch)
½ teaspoon fine sea salt
¼ teaspoon ground white pepper
pinch of caster (superfine) sugar
1 tablespoon light soy sauce
1 teaspoon sesame oil
1 tablespoon Shaoxing wine
1 large (US extra large) egg, beaten
1 tablespoon vegetable oil
250 g (9 oz) grated cheddar or mozzarella

FOR THE TOMATO SAUCE

1 tablespoon vegetable oil
1 small onion, finely diced
1 teaspoon finely chopped garlic
pinch of fine sea salt
pinch of ground white pepper
2 large tomatoes (about 200 g /7 oz), chopped into chunks
1 tablespoon tomato purée (paste)
2 heaped tablespoons tomato ketchup
1 teaspoon light soy sauce
½ teaspoon granulated sugar
100–150 ml (3½–5 fl oz/scant ½–scant ⅔ cup) water

FOR THE EGG FRIED RICE

1 tablespoon vegetable oil, plus extra as needed
2 large (US extra large) eggs, beaten with a pinch of salt and ground white or black pepper
½ teaspoon finely chopped fresh ginger root
½ teaspoon finely chopped garlic
250 g (9 oz/generous 1⅓ cups) cooked basmati rice (or a microwavable pouch)
½ teaspoon chicken stock powder
1 tablespoon light soy sauce

METHOD

1. Place the pork chops between two sheets of cling film (plastic wrap) and use a mallet or rolling pin to flatten them.
2. In a bowl, mix together the cornflour, salt, white pepper, sugar, soy sauce, sesame oil, Shaoxing wine and egg. Add the pork chops and stir to coat.
3. Next, make the tomato sauce. Heat the oil in a saucepan over a medium heat, then add the onion, garlic, salt and white pepper, and cook for 5 minutes until softened. If the onion and garlic start to catch, add a splash of water.
4. Now add the tomatoes, tomato purée, tomato ketchup, soy sauce and sugar. Cook for another couple of minutes, then add the water and cook for another minute.
5. While the sauce is cooking, cook the pork chops. Heat the vegetable oil in a wok or frying pan over a high heat and fry the chops for 3–5 minutes on each side until cooked through. Transfer to a plate and set aside.
6. In the same wok or pan, make the rice. Heat the oil over a high heat, add the eggs and cook for 2 minutes, swirling the pan every 15 seconds, so the egg fills the gaps to create a lightly cooked omelette. Move the egg to one side and add a little bit more oil, then fry the ginger and garlic for 1 minute until fragrant. Add the rice, stock powder and soy sauce. Toss for a couple of minutes, then break the egg into pieces and mix through the rice.
7. Preheat the grill (broiler). Pour the rice into the bottom of a heatproof dish, then layer half the sauce on top of the rice. Add the pork chops, then pour over the remaining sauce. Finally, top with the grated cheese.
8. Grill for 5 minutes until the cheese is brown and bubbly, then serve.

Granny's Steamed Soy Sauce Chicken Rice

This dish is really nostalgic for me. When I was a child, our granny came to stay with us when she was sick, and she stayed in my bedroom. I really enjoyed having her in the house as she used to tell me stories and she made food. One of the dishes she made was this simple but delicious chicken and rice dish. It was all cooked together in one pot: rice and chicken marinated in soy sauce, steamed together and served with green vegetables.

Serves 2
Prep: 5 minutes
Cook: 25 minutes

INGREDIENTS

400–500 g (14 oz–1 lb 2 oz) skinless and boneless chicken thighs, sliced
1 teaspoon cornflour (cornstarch)
1 tablespoon dark soy sauce
½ tablespoon light soy sauce, plus extra to serve
1 teaspoon sesame oil
pinch of ground white pepper
200 g (7 oz/1 cup) basmati rice, rinsed in cold water three times
300 ml (10 fl oz/1¼ cups) water
blanched green vegetables, to serve

METHOD

1. Put the sliced chicken in a bowl with the cornflour, dark and light soy sauces, sesame oil and white pepper. Mix to coat. Set aside.
2. Put the rice and water int a saucepan and bring to the boil. Cook for 3 minutes, then reduce the heat to a medium simmer and cook for a further 2 minutes. The rice should still be submerged in liquid.
3. Add the chicken on top in one layer, then cover with the lid (make sure it is tight-fitting, otherwise use foil). Simmer for 10–15 minutes until the chicken and rice are cooked.
4. To serve, drizzle with a little more light soy sauce and enjoy with some freshly blanched green vegetables.

Mushroom Curry

This is a nod to a Northern Irish Chinese takeaway curry. It is a cross between a chip shop curry sauce and a thick gravy made with a coconut base. It is one of the top sellers in our family takeaway and so many have asked for my mum's secret recipe. Unfortunately, the original recipe takes 12 hours to make, from the initial paste to the final sauce, so it is definitely not a recipe for those short of time or even this book! I have created a version that is super flavourful and very much like the real thing, which can be made in less time. I absolutely love mushrooms – they are so good in a curry.

Serves 2
Prep: 5 minutes
Cook: 20 minutes

INGREDIENTS

1 onion, diced
400 g (14 oz) mushrooms of your choice, chopped
1 tablespoon vegetable oil
1 tablespoon mild curry powder
1 star anise
1 teaspoon finely chopped fresh ginger root
1 teaspoon finely chopped garlic
1 heaped teaspoon vegetable stock powder or 1 vegetable stock cube, crumbled
200 ml (7 fl oz/scant 1 cup) coconut milk
large handful of fresh or frozen peas
1 tablespoon cornflour (cornstarch) mixed with 2 tablespoons water to make a paste
noodles or rice, to serve

METHOD

1. Bring a saucepan of water to the boil and blanch the onion and mushrooms for 1 minute, then drain and set aside.
2. Heat the oil in a wok over a medium heat. Add the curry powder, star anise, ginger and garlic and fry for about 1 minute until fragrant. Make sure the ginger and garlic don't burn. If they start to catch, add a splash of water.
3. Add the stock powder or cube and coconut milk. Mix well until combined, then simmer for 10 minutes.
4. Finally, add the onion, mushrooms and peas, stir and simmer for a further 5 minutes.
5. If you want a thicker sauce, reduce the heat, add the cornflour paste and stir it through. Bring the sauce to a boil and cook until thickened to your liking.
6. Remove the star anise, then serve with noodles or rice.

Honey Chilli Beef

Honey chilli beef and honey chilli chicken are Northern Irish takeaway classics. Thin strips of crispy coated beef or chicken in a sticky, spicy sauce – what's not to love? I have been asked time and time again for this recipe, so here it is.

Serves 2
Prep: 15 minutes
Cook: 15 minutes

INGREDIENTS

500 g (1 lb 2 oz) rump (sirloin) steak, cut into thin strips against the grain
1 teaspoon cornflour (cornstarch)
pinch of fine sea salt
pinch of ground white pepper
1 tablespoon light soy sauce
1 teaspoon sesame oil
1 onion, sliced
1 green (bell) pepper, sliced
vegetable oil, for frying
sliced spring onions (scallions), to serve

FOR THE SAUCE

2 garlic cloves, finely chopped
1 red chilli, sliced, and deseeded if you don't want it as spicy
2 tablespoons light soy sauce
160 g (5½ oz/scant ½ cup) honey (not flavoured)
60 ml (2 fl oz/¼ cup) distilled white vinegar
pinch of fine sea salt

FOR THE BATTER COATING

2 medium (US large) eggs, beaten
8 tablespoons plain (all-purpose) flour
8 tablespoons cornflour (cornstarch)
pinch of fine sea salt
pinch of ground white pepper

METHOD

1. Preheat the oven to 180°C fan/200°C/400°F/Gas 6.
2. Put the beef strips in a bowl and add the cornflour, salt, white pepper, soy sauce and sesame oil. Mix to coat, then set aside to marinate for at least 5 minutes.
3. Meanwhile, mix together all the ingredients for the sauce in a bowl.
4. Coat the beef. Put the beaten egg in a dish and put the flour, cornflour, salt and white pepper in a separate dish. Toss the beef through the egg, then through the flour mixture.
5. Pour about 1 cm (½ in) of oil into a heavy-based saucepan over a high heat. Place the end of a wooden spoon in the oil – if bubbles sizzle around the spoon, the oil is hot enough.
6. Shake off excess flour from the beef strips, then carefully drop a handful into the oil, spreading them out as you do so. Cook for 1–2 minutes on each side, then transfer to a wire rack set over a baking tray (pan) and continue with the remaining beef. Make sure you fry the beef strips in small batches, so as not to overcrowd the pan, and be careful not to overcook them. Place the beef in the oven to keep warm and crisp.
7. Tip the hot oil into a bowl (wait until it is cold and filter out the floaty bits with some paper towels and reuse another time).
8. Add a little vegetable oil to a wok over a high heat, then fry the onion and peppers for 1 minute until browned.
9. Add the sauce along with a splash of water to loosen it. Let the sauce bubble away for 3–4 minutes until sticky.
10. Now add the beef strips and quickly toss, so everything is coated in the sauce. Cook for 2 minutes and serve.

Lemon Chicken

This has always been a big takeaway favourite. I have made it with chicken thighs because I think they're juicier, but you can use breast meat if you prefer. I also shallow-fried the chicken pieces, but you can deep-fry them or even cook them in an air fryer.

Serves 2
Prep: 5 minutes
Cook: 25 minutes

INGREDIENTS

400 g (14 oz) skinless and boneless chicken thighs
4 heaped tablespoons plain (all-purpose) flour
4 heaped tablespoons cornflour (cornstarch)
1 large (US extra large) egg, beaten
90 ml (3 fl oz/⅓ cup) vegetable oil
fine sea salt and ground white pepper

FOR THE SAUCE

100 ml (3½ fl oz/scant ½ cup) fresh lemon juice (from about 2 lemons)
3 tablespoons caster (superfine) sugar
2 teaspoons cornflour (cornstarch)
200 ml (7 fl oz/scant 1 cup) water

TO SERVE

shredded lettuce
rice or noodles
lemon slices

METHOD

1. Season the chicken with salt. Combine the flours in a bowl and put the beaten egg in another bowl. Toss the chicken in the flours, then plunge it into the beaten egg and back into the flour mix, so it is fully covered. This will create the crunchy exterior.
2. Heat the vegetable oil in a wok over a high heat, then fry the chicken for 8–10 minutes until golden and cooked on both sides. Remove and place on paper towels to drain.
3. Next, make the lemon sauce. Combine everything in a small saucepan and whisk until combined, then gently bring to the boil until the sauce becomes thick and glossy. Then pour through a sieve (strainer).
4. Slice the chicken, then serve on a bed of lettuce and rice or noodles with the sauce and topped with lemon slices.

Orange Chicken

This could not be easier to make, and you don't even need an orange – just cordial (this is how it is made in our family takeaway). If you don't have that, fresh orange juice works well, but you will need to balance it with some sugar or sweetener.

Serves 2
Prep: 10 minutes
Cook: 20 minutes

INGREDIENTS

12 chicken breast mini fillets
good pinch of fine sea salt
good pinch of ground white pepper
1 medium orange, half cut into quarter slices and the other half squeezed
6–8 tablespoons double-strength orange squash (cordial)
400 ml (14 fl oz/scant 2 cups) water
2 tablespoons cornflour (cornflour) mixed with 4 tablespoons water to make a paste
oil spray, as needed

FOR THE EGG MIX

2 large (US extra large) eggs, beaten
2 teaspoon cornflour (cornstarch)

FOR THE FLOUR MIX

8 heaped tablespoons self-raising (self-rising) flour
4 heaped tablespoons cornflour (cornstarch)
big pinch of fine sea salt

METHOD

1. Combine the ingredients for the egg mix in one bowl and the ingredients for the flour mix in a separate bowl.
2. Coat the chicken fillets in the egg mix, then coat them in the flour mix.
3. Preheat an air fryer to 200°C (400°F). You can also shallow-fry, deep-fry or oven-bake the chicken fillets until crispy and golden. (The chicken fillets will take about 8–10 minutes to shallow-fry.)
4. Spray the air fryer basket with some oil, then add the coated chicken and spray with a bit more oil. Cook in the air fryer for 10–12 minutes until crispy and golden, flipping halfway through with tongs.
5. Meanwhile, make the orange sauce. Combine the orange juice, squash, water and cornflour paste in a small saucepan and whisk until combined. Gently bring the sauce to the boil until it becomes thick and glossy. If you prefer a thinner sauce, add more water.
6. Place the chicken pieces on a serving dish, then serve with some orange slices and sauce.

King Prawn Spice Bag

The spice bag is an Irish classic! Chips (fries), crispy chicken, (bell) peppers and onions tossed in a chilli spice mix. In essence, it's a Chinese takeaway salt and pepper dish mashed together with a chippy chicken and chips! To speed things up, I'm using oven chips cooked in an air fryer and king prawns (jumbo shrimp), but you can make your own chips if you have more time. You could also use breaded prawns or scampi (langoustine tails) – just cook according to the packet instructions.

Serves 2
Prep: 10 minutes
Cook: 15 minutes

INGREDIENTS

200 g (7 oz) frozen oven chips (fries)
200 g (7 oz) raw king prawns (jumbo shrimp), butterflied and digestive trac removed
1 tablespoon cornflour (cornstarch)
good pinch of fine sea salt
good pinch of ground white pepper
1 tablespoon vegetable oil
1 onion, sliced
1 (bell) pepper, sliced
1 heaped teaspoon finely chopped garlic
1 tablespoon finely chopped fresh ginger root
1 red or green chilli, finely sliced (use more if you like food spicier), and deseeded if you don't want it as spicy
sliced spring onions (scallions), to serve

FOR THE SALT AND CHILLI SPICE MIX

1 teaspoon Chinese five-spice powder
½ tablespoon fine sea salt
½ teaspoon ground white pepper
½ tablespoon caster (superfine) sugar
½ teaspoon dried red chilli (hot pepper) flakes

METHOD

1. Cook the chips in an air fryer according to the packet instructions (or in the oven or a deep fryer).
2. Combine all the ingredients for the spice mix in a small bowl.
3. Pat the prawns dry with paper towels, put in a bowl and dust with the cornflour, salt and white pepper. Heat the oil in a wok or large frying pan over a high heat, then add the prawns and stir-fry for a couple of minutes until they curl up and just turn pink. Remove and set aside.
4. Add the onion to the pan and cook for a couple of minutes, then add the pepper and cook for a further few minutes.
5. Add the garlic, ginger and chilli and fry for a couple of minutes until the ginger and garlic are fragrant.
6. Add half the spice mix and stir it through the vegetables, then add the prawns and chips and toss everything together until coated in the spice mix. Taste and add the rest of the spice mix if you want more flavour. The spice bag is now ready to eat!

MEILLEUR AVANT
維他
VLT
TEA DRINK

Duck and Pineapple

Duck is a widely used Chinese ingredient. Pairing it with pineapple, however, is not traditional, but this is another takeaway classic. This dish is not unlike sweet and sour, but extra layers of flavour come from the ginger, garlic, soy sauce and pineapple.

Serves 2
Prep: 10 minutes
Cook: 20 minutes

INGREDIENTS

2 duck breasts, skin on
1 small carrot, peeled and sliced on the diagonal
1 small onion, cut into chunks
1 small green (bell) pepper, cut into chunks
1 small garlic clove, sliced
10 g (½ oz) fresh ginger root, sliced
4 tablespoons tomato ketchup
2 tablespoons rice vinegar, distilled white vinegar or white wine vinegar
2 heaped tablespoons granulated sugar
2 tablespoons light soy sauce
200 g (7 oz) fresh or canned pineapple, cut into chunks
fine sea salt and ground white pepper

METHOD

1. Pat the duck breasts dry with paper towels, then score the skin and rub it with a pinch of salt. Place the breasts in a cold frying pan, skin side down. Bring to a medium heat and cook for 10–12 minutes until the skin is golden, draining and reserving any excess fat now and again, then flip and cook for about 3 minutes to colour the flesh side. Remove the duck and set aside to rest.
2. Now add the carrot, onion and pepper along with a splash of water and cook for about 2 minutes.
3. Next, add 1 tablespoon of the rendered duck fat to the pan, add the garlic and ginger and fry for about 1 minute until aromatic.
4. Now add the ketchup, your choice of vinegar, sugar and soy sauce and let them bubble for a couple of minutes. Add the pineapple and allow everything to caramelize. This will take another couple of minutes over a high heat.
5. Slice the duck breasts against the grain, then add the sauce and vegetables. Taste and adjust the seasoning as needed, then serve.

Char Siu Chicken and Eggs

My mum used to make this for us using char siu pork, as she made it for our takeaway. *Char sui* means 'fork roasted', but the dish is known as Cantonese-style roasted barbecue pork. Making char siu chicken is super quick and easy. It can be made in advance and the extras saved for dishes like this or even sandwiches.

Serves 2
Prep: 5 minutes
Cook: 20 minutes

INGREDIENTS

400 g (14 oz) chicken breast mini fillets
1 tablespoon black treacle (molasses)
1 tablespoon runny honey
2 tablespoons hoisin sauce
1 teaspoon dark soy sauce
1 teaspoon Chinese five-spice powder
1 teaspoon oyster sauce
1 teaspoon red food colouring (optional)
6 large (US extra large) eggs
1 teaspoon sesame oil
½ teaspoon light soy sauce
1 tablespoon vegetable oil
fine sea salt and ground white pepper

TO SERVE

sliced spring onions (scallions)
rice

METHOD

1. Put the chicken in a bowl with the treacle, honey, hoisin sauce, dark soy sauce, Chinese five-spice powder, oyster sauce and food colouring (if using). Mix together, then set aside to marinate for at least 5 minutes. This can be done in advance and even the day before.
2. To cook in an air fryer, preheat the air fryer to 200°C (400°F), then cook the chicken for 10 minutes until cooked through and charred in places.
3. Alternatively, preheat the grill (broiler) to high and cook the chicken for 5–6 minutes on each side.
4. Once cooked, slice the chicken and set aside.
5. Beat the eggs in a bowl with the sesame oil, light soy sauce, and a pinch of salt and white pepper.
6. Heat the vegetable oil in a wok or frying pan over a high heat and add the beaten egg mixture, swirling the pan every 15 seconds, so the egg fills the gaps. Once the egg is about three-quarters cooked, add the chicken and fold it in. Stir-fry the chicken and eggs for a minute or so, but be careful not to overcook them.
7. Serve sprinkled with spring onions to garnish alongside a steaming bowl of rice.

Honey and Soy Sauce Chicken Thighs

This recipe came about through having two very hungry children who love flavoursome chicken! All this dish needs is three ingredients and 30 minutes of your time. The thighs are crispy, sticky and delicious and are perfect as a starter (appetizer), with rice or noodles, or on their own!

Serves 4
Prep: 5 minutes
Cook: 20–25 minutes

INGREDIENTS

6 chicken thighs, skin on
4 tablespoons honey
4 tablespoons light soy sauce
pinch of fine sea salt
pinch of ground white pepper

METHOD

1. Preheat an air fryer to 200°C (400°F) or the oven to 180°C fan/200°C/400°F/Gas 6.
2. Put the chicken thighs in a bowl, then add the honey, soy sauce, salt and white pepper and massage the sauce into the chicken thighs. Flip the chicken thighs, so the flesh is sitting in the marinade (skin side up), then set aside to marinate for at least 5 minutes. The chicken can be prepared in advance, and even the night before (in which case, store in the refrigerator).
3. Place the chicken thighs skin side down in the air fryer basket, reserving any leftover marinade. Cook for 10 minutes, then flip over, brush with the reserved marinade and cook for a further 10 minutes. If the thighs are particularly large, they may need an extra couple of minutes – cut into them to check they are cooked through.
4. To cook in the oven, cut two slices into each chicken thigh down to the bone, then place in a roasting tin and brush with the excess marinade. Roast in the oven for 25 minutes, then serve.

Crunchy Chicken Stir-fry

You cannot go wrong with a chicken stir-fry and jazzing the dish up with some crunchy vegetables gives it more depth. I love all these vegetables and they are often in my refrigerator, so it's easy to quickly blanch them and then cook them in a light sauce to serve with a bowl of rice.

Serves 2
Prep: 5 minutes
Cook: 15–20 minutes

INGREDIENTS

1 large chicken breast (about 300 g/10½ oz), finely sliced
1 teaspoon cornflour (cornstarch)
1 tablespoon plus 2 teaspoons light soy sauce
1 teaspoon sesame oil
100 g (3½ oz) green beans, trimmed
100 g (3½ oz) mangetout (snow peas)
1 large carrot, peeled and sliced on the diagonal
1 tablespoon vegetable oil
½ teaspoon chicken stock powder or ½ chicken stock cube, crumbled
200 ml (7 fl oz/scant 1 cup) water
fine sea salt and ground white pepper
1 tablespoon cornflour (cornstarch) paste (see page 17)

METHOD

1. Put the chicken in a bowl with the cornflour, 1 tablespoon of soy sauce and sesame oil and mix well, then set to one side.
2. Bring a saucepan of water to the boil and blanch the green beans, mangetout and carrot for 1 minute, then drain.
3. Heat a wok or saucepan over a high heat, add the vegetable oil and fry the chicken for a couple of minutes, then flip and cook for another couple of minutes until just browned. Add the veggies and stir-fry for a minute.
4. Add the 2 teaspoons of soy sauce, the chicken stock powder or cube and the water, stir, taste and season as needed with salt and white pepper.
5. Reduce the heat and add the cornflour paste, then mix and allow to bubble for another couple of minutes until thickened before serving. If you would like the stir-fry saucier, you can add a bit more water (and adjust the seasoning accordingly).
6. Serve with some steaming hot basmati rice, noodles or as is.

Chinese Pulled Chicken

We love pulled pork and pulled beef in my house, but I wanted a change and had chicken in the refrigerator, so I thought I could try a really quick version with that instead. Not only does chicken cook quickly but it also shreds more easily if poached than both pork and beef. Serve with salad, rice or noodles and some steamed veggies. It's great for packed lunches, too.

Serves 2
Prep: 5 minutes
Cook: 20 minutes

INGREDIENTS

1 teaspoon vegetable oil
2 teaspoons grated garlic
2 teaspoons grated fresh ginger root
2 tablespoons dark soy sauce
½ teaspoon chicken stock powder
pinch of ground white pepper
2 chicken breasts (about 400 g/14 oz)
200 ml (7 fl oz/scant 1 cup) water
1 tablespoon cornflour (cornstarch) mixed with 2 tablespoons water to make a paste
1 teaspoon sesame oil

TO SERVE

toasted sesame seeds
sliced spring onions (scallions)
sliced red chillies

METHOD

1. Heat the vegetable oil in a small saucepan over a high heat and fry the garlic and ginger for a couple of minutes until fragrant.
2. Add the soy sauce, chicken stock powder and white pepper, then add the chicken breasts and flip them around to coat thoroughly in the seasonings.
3. Add the water, cover and reduce the heat to medium. Simmer for 10 minutes, then flip the breasts and cook for a further 10 minutes before removing from the heat.
4. Once cooked, remove the chicken from the pan and use two forks to shred the meat.
5. Add the cornflour paste to the cooking liquid in the pan and stir it through, then bring to the boil and cook until the sauce thickens.
6. Toss the chicken through the sauce until it is well coated, then drizzle in the sesame oil.
7. Serve sprinkled with sesame seeds, spring onions and chillies.

Sweet Hoisin Chicken Skewers

I love the hawker street food markets in Hong Kong and the variety of different skewered barbecue meats you can find there is unreal. There are so many flavours that I had a go at playing around with what I had in my cupboards. I spotted the hoisin sauce, which is used less frequently in my house, and thought it would caramelize well. The experiment was successful and this dish turned out to be an absolute crowd pleaser. The chicken can be marinated the night before to make it even more packed with flavour.

Serves 4
Prep: 10 minutes
Cook: 15 minutes

INGREDIENTS

1 tablespoon hoisin sauce
1 tablespoon honey
1 teaspoon dark soy sauce
1 teaspoon sesame oil
1 teaspoon cornflour (cornstarch)
400 g (14 oz) skinless, boneless chicken thighs, sliced in half lengthways, or mini fillets or whole breasts, sliced into chunks

METHOD

1. Combine all the ingredients in a bowl and leave to marinate for at least 10 minutes.
2. Thread the chicken onto skewers, stretching out each one on the skewer. If you are using wooden skewers, makes sure to soak them in water for at least 30 minutes beforehand to stop them from burning.
3. To cook, preheat an air fryer to 200°C (400°F) or the grill (broiler) to 220°C (425°F). Cook in the air fryer for 7–8 minutes, flipping halfway through, or under the grill for 10–12 minutes, also flipping halfway through.

Chicken and Sweetcorn Rice Bowl

Another childhood favourite of mine – chicken and sweetcorn. There is just something so comforting about this topping a big bowl of rice.

Serves 4
Prep: 5 minutes
Cook: 20 minutes

INGREDIENTS

400 g (14 oz) chicken thighs or breast fillets, cut into bite-size pieces
2 teaspoons light soy sauce
1 teaspoon cornflour (cornstarch)
1 tablespoon vegetable oil
1 small white onion, finely chopped
½ teaspoon garlic granules
pinch of fine sea salt
400 g (14 oz) tin of creamed sweetcorn
2 tablespoons tinned or frozen sweetcorn
1 teaspoon chicken stock powder or 1 chicken stock cube, crumbled
large pinch of ground white pepper
100–200 ml (3½–7 fl oz/scant ½–scant 1 cup) water
1 teaspoon cornflour (cornstarch) mixed with 2 teaspoons water to make a paste
1 large (US extra large) egg, beaten
1 teaspoon sesame oil

METHOD

1. Put the chicken pieces in a bowl with the soy sauce and cornflour, mix well and set aside to marinate for at least 5 minutes.
2. Heat the vegetable oil in a wok or large frying pan over a high heat and fry the chicken for 2–3 minutes until browned. Transfer the chicken to a bowl and set to one side. Do not clean the wok or pan.
3. Add the onion to the wok or pan and fry over a medium heat for 5 minutes, then add the garlic granules, salt and a splash of water (this helps to deglaze the pan).
4. Cover and cook for 2–3 minutes until the onions have softened. Add a splash more water if the onions start to catch.
5. Add the creamed sweetcorn, sweetcorn, chicken stock powder or cube, chicken pieces, white pepper and 100 ml (3½ fl oz/scant ½ cup) water and cook for about 1 minute. If you like a lot of sauce, add the rest of the water (or more). If you do add more water, you will need to add the cornflour paste. To do this, reduce the heat, add the cornflour paste too and stir it through. Bring the sauce to a boil and cook until thickened. Cook this for a further 8–10 minutes.
6. Now carefully drizzle the beaten egg around the wok or pan in a continuous stream. This will create ribbons or flecks of egg through the dish.
7. Finish by drizzling the sesame oil around the edge of the hot wok or pan, so the oil becomes nice and fragrant.
8. Season to taste and serve in bowls over hot basmati rice.

XO Mussels

I love mussels and they are a widely available ingredient for me in Northern Ireland. They are also extremely good value for money. XO sauce is a seafood-based condiment and it adds so much flavour to these mussels. It was invented in Hong Kong by a top chef in the Peninsula Hotel. Even though it is named after a Cognac, it does not contain any alcohol. Rather the name reflects the luxurious seafood produce used in the sauce.

Serves 4
Prep: 20 minutes
Cook: 10 minutes

INGREDIENTS

1 kg (2 lb 4 oz) mussels
50 g (1¾ oz) XO sauce (including some oil from the jar)
1 small onion, sliced
2 teaspoons finely chopped garlic
1 tablespoon Shaoxing wine
sliced spring onions (scallions), to serve

METHOD

1. Put the mussels in a bowl of water and leave to soak for 15 minutes, then remove any beards. Transfer to a colander and rinse again. Leave to drain in the colander.
2. Heat a wok over a high heat, add the XO sauce, onion and garlic and fry for 2–3 minutes until fragrant.
3. Add the mussels, then the Shaoxing wine and stir everything together.
4. Cover and cook for about 5 minutes, then stir and cook for a further 2 minutes. Finally stir again and cook for another minute.
5. Discard any mussels that have not opened at all.
6. Serve sprinkled with some spring onions.

Crispy Pork Chops with Salad Cream

This is a very popular dish in Hong Kong. It evolved from a baked pork chop rice dish without the tomato sauce, and instead uses Hong Kong's favourite condiment: salad cream. My children got to try this dish in 2023 when we visited Hong Kong and have requested it ever since. If you don't have panko breadcrumbs, you can rip up a large tortilla wrap into small pieces and blitz it to crumbs in a food processor.

Serves 2
Prep: 10 minutes
Cook: 15 minutes

INGREDIENTS

2 boneless pork chops, rind trimmed off
(or 2 pork shoulder steaks)
1 heaped teaspoon cornflour (cornstarch)
1 teaspoon sesame oil
1 teaspoon light soy sauce
1 teaspoon Shaoxing wine
1 large (US extra large) egg
¼ teaspoon fine sea salt
pinch of ground white pepper
4 heaped tablespoons panko breadcrumbs
3 tablespoons vegetable oil
salad cream, to serve

METHOD

1. Place the pork chops or steaks between two sheets of cling film (plastic wrap) and use a mallet or rolling pin to flatten them, then cut them both in half.
2. Put the pork in a bowl along with the cornflour, sesame oil, soy sauce, Shaoxing wine, egg, salt and white pepper. Mix well, then set aside to marinate for at least 10 minutes.
3. Put the breadcrumbs on a plate. Once the pork is marinated, coat it in the breadcrumbs until fully covered.
4. Heat the vegetable oil in a frying pan over a medium heat and fry the pork for 6–7 minutes on each side until crisp and golden brown.
5. Cut the crispy pork into 1 cm (½ in) strips and serve with salad cream.

Pork and Beansprout Stir-Fry

I think beansprouts are underrated. I love the texture and flavour they add to a dish and they literally cook in a flash. You can serve this stir-fry with rice or noodles, but I really enjoy it as it is.

Serves 2
Prep: 10 minutes
Cook: 15 minutes

INGREDIENTS

250 g (9 oz) boneless pork chops, finely sliced
1 tablespoon plus 1 teaspoon light soy sauce
1 heaped teaspoon cornflour (cornstarch)
1 tablespoon Shaoxing wine
1 tablespoon vegetable oil
2 spring onions (scallions), white and green parts separated and finely sliced
125 g (4½ oz) chestnut (cremini) mushrooms, sliced
1 tablespoon oyster sauce
400 g (14 oz) beansprouts
1 teaspoon sesame oil
fine sea salt and ground white pepper

METHOD

1. Put the pork, 1 teaspoon of the soy sauce, cornflour and Shaoxing wine in a bowl and mix well. Let the pork marinate for 10 minutes.
2. Heat the vegetable oil in a wok over a high heat and fry the pork slices for 2 minutes until browned, then add the white parts of the spring onions.
3. Add the mushrooms and fry for 2 minutes, then add the remaining tablespoon of soy sauce, the oyster sauce and beansprouts. Drizzle the sesame oil around the edge of the wok.
4. Cook for a further 3 minutes.
5. Serve topped with the spring onions greens.

Duck with Ginger and Spring Onions

This dish is an extremely traditional Hakka recipe that is usually slow-cooked, making it very flavoursome. However, time is always at a premium, so I decided to experiment with slicing up the duck breasts and kind of working backwards, making sure I got a good, tasty sauce and then adding the duck again . . . and it worked!

Serves 4
Prep: 10 minutes
Cook: 20 minutes

INGREDIENTS

500 g (1 lb 2 oz) duck breasts (about 2 large breasts), sliced
1 teaspoon cornflour (cornstarch), plus extra cornflour paste if needed (see page 17)
1 tablespoon plus 1 teaspoon dark soy sauce
1 tablespoon Shaoxing wine
1 tablespoon vegetable oil
30 g (1 oz) fresh ginger root, grated
3 spring onions (scallions), white parts finely sliced and green parts chopped into 5 cm (2 in) pieces
2 cubes of fermented red tofu (bean curd)
½ teaspoon chicken stock powder
200 ml (7 fl oz/scant 1 cup) water
fine sea salt and large pinch ground white pepper

METHOD

1. Put the sliced duck, cornflour, 1 teaspoon of the dark soy sauce, white pepper and Shaoxing wine in a bowl, mix well and set aside to marinate for at least 10 minutes.
2. Once marinated, heat the vegetable oil in a wok over a high heat and flash-fry the duck for a couple of minutes, then transfer to a bowl and set aside. Do not clean the wok.
3. Add the ginger and the white parts of the spring onions to the wok and fry for about 1 minute until fragrant, then add the fermented tofu, the remaining tablespoon of soy sauce, stock powder and water and mash down the bean curd until it disintegrates into the sauce. Simmer for 10 minutes.
4. Finally, add the duck to the sauce and stir, then taste and season accordingly.
5. If you want a thicker sauce, reduce the heat, add some cornflour paste, 1 teaspoon at a time, and stir it through. Bring the sauce to a boil and cook until thickened.
6. Toss through the spring onion greens. Serve.

Beef Steak and Juicy Tomato Sauce

This was another favourite of mine growing up: soft, sweet tomatoes with melt-in-the-mouth beef. Such a simple pairing of ingredients made into something so yummy. Perfect over a bowl of rice.

Serves 4
Prep: 10 minutes
Cook: 15 minutes

INGREDIENTS

400 g (14 oz) rump (sirloin) steak, sliced against the grain and diagonally (large, flat, thin slices)
2 teaspoons cornflour (cornstarch)
1 teaspoon sesame oil
1 tablespoon light soy sauce
1 tablespoon Shaoxing wine
2 tablespoons vegetable oil
1 onion, sliced
2 garlic cloves, finely chopped or grated
10 g (½ oz) fresh ginger root, peeled and finely sliced
3 tomatoes, each chopped into 8 segments
fine sea salt and ground white pepper
sliced spring onions (scallions), to serve

FOR THE SAUCE

4 tablespoons tomato ketchup
2 heaped teaspoons caster (superfine) sugar
1 teaspoon light soy sauce
1 teaspoon sesame oil
100 ml (3½ fl oz/scant ½ cup) water

METHOD

1. Put the steak slices in a bowl with the cornflour, sesame oil, soy sauce and Shaoxing wine. Mix well, then set aside to marinate for at least 10 minutes.
2. Heat the vegetable oil in a wok over a high heat, then flash-fry the beef in two batches, for a couple of minutes each. Transfer to a bowl and set aside. Do not clean the wok.
3. Add the onion, garlic and ginger and fry for about 1 minute until fragrant.
4. Now make the sauce. Add the ketchup and sugar to the wok, stir through and allow to caramelize for a couple of minutes. Then add the soy sauce, sesame oil and water and simmer for another couple of minutes.
5. Throw in the tomatoes, mix through and allow them to just soften – this will only take about 2–3 minutes.
6. Season to taste with salt and white pepper. You may want it tangier, so add more ketchup!
7. Serve sprinkled with spring onion.

Mango Pancakes

Here's an iconic dim sum dessert from Hong Kong, in which the bright yellow pancake reflects the golden mango inside. The origin of this dish is unknown, but it is widely served at dim sum and dessert houses in Hong Kong. I have altered the recipe a little bit as I didn't want to use yellow food colouring to give it that nearly neon-yellow colour, but if you want to give it the characteristic colour, then add a pinch of ground turmeric. I have also diced up the mango instead of using a whole piece, as otherwise I find it really hard to eat the pancake without this going all over the place!

Serves 2
Prep: 5 minutes
Cook: 25 minutes

INGREDIENTS

4 tablespoons plain (all-purpose) flour
1½ tablespoons cornflour (cornstarch)
1 tablespoon caster (superfine) sugar
125 ml (4 fl oz/½ cup) whole milk
1 large (US extra large) egg, at room temperature
3–4 drops yellow food colouring or a pinch of ground turmeric (optional)
1 teaspoon vanilla extract
1 heaped teaspoon unsalted butter, melted
1 small carton (250 ml/8 fl oz/1 cup) of double (heavy) or whipping cream
2 tablespoons condensed milk
1 large ripe mango, diced

METHOD

1. To make the pancakes, combine the flour, cornflour, sugar, milk, egg, food colouring or turmeric (if using) and vanilla extract in a food processor and blend until smooth, then pour through a sieve (strainer) into a jug (pitcher).
2. Add the melted butter to the pancake mixture and stir through.
3. Heat a non-stick frying pan over a high heat, then reduce the heat to medium just before you make the first pancake. Pour about a quarter of the mixture into the pan and swirl it around to ensure it spreads out evenly to coat the bottom of the pan.
4. Now turn the heat to low, then, once the edges start to curl away from the pan, lift the pancake out with a spatula and place on a clean dish towel, wrapping it up to keep it soft and pliable. Repeat with the remaining mixture to make four or five pancakes.
5. Whisk the double or whipping cream with the condensed milk until soft peaks form.
6. Place 1–2 tablespoons of the diced mango into the centre of each pancake, then top with the sweetened cream.
7. Fold the sides of the pancake inwards, then fold over the bottom and roll it up to enclose everything. Repeat for the remaining pancakes.
8. Enjoy straight away.

Mochi aka *Lau Mai Chi*

When I was growing up, mochi (little Chinese pastries) were often made by my mum and Auntie Linda. You can enjoy many different fillings in them. In Hong Kong, it is popular to flavour them with sesame, peanut and sugar. You can also add desiccated coconut to them. Other filling suggestions include fresh mango slices and peanut butter frozen into balls before wrapping up in the dough.

Makes 8 mochi
Prep: 5 minutes
Cook: 20 minutes

INGREDIENTS

40 g (1½ oz/¼ cup) roasted peanuts, roughly chopped
25 g (1 oz/2½ tablespoons) toasted white or black sesame seeds, roughly chopped
25 g (1 oz) sugar
150 g (5½ oz/generous ¾ cup) glutinous rice flour
1½ tablespoons cornflour (cornstarch)
1½ tablespoons vegetable or sunflower oil
150 ml (5 fl oz/scant ⅔ cup) water

METHOD

1. Combine the peanuts, sesame seeds and sugar in a bowl and mix well.
2. Dry-fry 50 g (1¾ oz/scant ¼ cup) of the glutinous rice flour in a frying pan over a medium heat for a couple of minutes until it turns the slightest golden colour, then remove and set aside.
3. Combine the remaining glutinous rice flour, cornflour, vegetable or sunflower oil, and water in a bowl and whisk until smooth. Place a plate on top or cover with cling film (plastic wrap) and microwave for 2 minutes on high, then mix and microwave again for a further 2 minutes.
4. Put on a pair of rubber gloves (the dough will be hot) and knead it on a clean, oiled surface for 3–4 minutes. Alternatively, grease the inside of a freezer bag with oil and knead the dough inside it.
5. Squeeze the dough between your thumb and index finger to form eight equal balls, then dust them with the toasted rice flour.
6. Roll each ball into a disc approximately 10 cm (4 in) wide. Fill each mochi with about 1 teaspoon of the nut mix filling, then crimp the edges to seal them together and flip over. Another way to fill the mochi is to place the dough discs over the holes of a muffin tin (pan).
7. Dust the filled mochi with a little more toasted rice flour (this stops them sticking together), then serve.
8. Mochi are best eaten on the day of preparation but can be kept for a few days in an airtight container at room temperature or, if made using fresh mango, in the refrigerator.

NOTE

If you do not have a microwave, you can use a steamer instead. Brush a heatproof bowl that fits in the steamer and is at least 3–4 cm (1¼–1½ indeep with oil. Pour the glutinous rice flour mixture into the bowl, steam for 12–15 minutes, then carry on with step 4.

Mango Sago

Mango sago became popular in the 1980s in Hong Kong. Sago are translucent, jelly-like pearls, similar to the tapioca pearls in bubble tea, and add texture to any dish. Mango is one of the most common flavours that goes with sago, but adding other fruits like pomelo pieces or strawberries can also make for a very tasty treat.

Serves 2
Prep: 5 minutes
Cook: 20 minutes

INGREDIENTS

1 litre (34 fl oz/4¼ cups) water
2 tablespoons uncooked sago pearls
200 g (7 oz) mango pieces in syrup
100 ml (3½ fl oz/scant ½ cup) coconut milk
3 tablespoons condensed milk, plus extra to serve
1 teaspoon vanilla extract

TO SERVE

fresh or tinned mango
pomelo pieces
strawberries

METHOD

1. Pour the water into a saucepan and bring to the boil, then carefully scatter the sago pearls into the vigorously boiling water. Lower the heat to medium and simmer for 15–20 minutes until the pearls become translucent. Once the pearls are ready, pour into a sieve (strainer) over the sink and rinse with cold water. Set aside in the sieve.
2. Meanwhile, make the mango 'soup'. Put the mango pieces with some of their syrup in a food processor along with the coconut milk, condensed milk and vanilla extract. Blend thoroughly until smooth.
3. Once the pearls are ready, combine the 'mango soup' with the sago, then divide between two bowls.
4. Serve topped with fruit and an extra drizzle of condensed milk, if you like.

ABOUT THE AUTHOR

Suzie Lee is a Chinese cook, the 2020 winner of BBC's *Best Home Cook* and the presenter of four series of *Suzie Lee's Home Cook Hero* and *Suzie Lee's Great Food Made Simple*. Brought up by her Hong Kong parents in Northern Ireland, Suzie was taught to cook by her mum, Celia, who sadly passed away when she was just 16. Even before winning *Best Home Cook*, Suzie was always being asked for her recipes and top tips in the kitchen. Suzie gives demonstrations at a range of regional and national food shows around the UK and has worked with a leading supermarket in Northern Ireland to develop a range of brand-new ready meals. This is Suzie's third cookbook.

ACKNOWLEDGEMENTS

This cookbook is inspired by my Mum, who unfortunately is no longer with us. My Mum has been my inspiration in all areas of life, she is the woman who gave me my grit and determination and, most importantly, is responsible for my love of food. She was the queen of rustling up dishes to feed her hungry family. So thank you Mum for showing me how!

Thank you to all of you who asked for these recipes, dishes that are a mish mash of things I grew up eating as well as ones that use up ingredients I have to hand to feed my family.

Thank you to Stevie, my hubby, who is ever patient and my voice of reason. He has been behind me every step of the way and without his support I would not have achieved half of what I have now.

My two rascals, Zander and Odie, for being brutal food critics. It has been a blast getting true and honest feedback from them. They have quite the palate but I am very grateful that they enjoy their food. It makes my life way easier!

To my siblings, Angela, Winnie, Veronica, Timmy, as well as Dad, who all had input in this book.

To my top food testers, Gillian Boyd, Jonny Baxter, Jill Caskey and Rachel Scott, your genuine opinions were so helpful.

Anne Kibel, my fab agent who always champions me and believes in me even when I don't! She saw the importance of me wanting to explore my food heritage in both of my cultures (Chinese and Northern Irish) and this third book has allowed me to be comfortable in 'fusion' dishes.

Lynne and Ivan Arbuthnot (my In-laws), Elizabeth Ramsey, The Scott Family, Rachel and Matt Fraser, who have been my support network throughout this writing process. I am indebted to them for all the pickups, drop offs, babysitting when I have been writing these recipes. Thank you from the bottom of my heart!

Kate Burkett from Quadrille, thank you for having the confidence in me and publishing this cookbook.

Uyen Luu and Clare Lewington for the wonderful photography, my food team of Sam Dixon, Lu Cottle, Sam Wong and Allegra D'Agostini. Thank you to Hannah Wilkinson for prop styling and the Team at Evi-O for making it all come together; the book is just so vibrant and fun.

Thank you!

INDEX

F

G

H

I

L

M

N

T

V

W

X

Quadrille, Penguin Random House UK, One Embassy Gardens, 8 Viaduct Gardens, London SW11 7BW

Quadrille Publishing Limited is part of the Penguin Random House group of companies whose addresses can be found at globalpenguinrandomhouse.com

Published by Quadrille in 2026
www.penguin.co.uk

A CIP catalogue record for this book is available from the British Library

ISBN 9781837833801
10 9 8 7 6 5 4 3 2 1

Managing Director, Publishing
Sarah Lavelle

Editorial Director
Sophie Allen

Senior Commissioning Editor
Kate Burkett

Copy Editor
Lucy Kingett

Proofreader
Caroline West

Indexer
Cathy Heath

Designer
Evi O

Photographer
Uyen Luu

Photographer Assistant
Clare Lewington

Food Stylist
Sam Dixon

Food Stylist Assistants
Lu Cottle, Sam Wong and Allegra D'agostini

Prop Stylist
Hannah Wilkinson

Head of Production
Stephen Lang

Senior Production Controller
Martina Georgieva

Colour reproduction by p2d
Printed in China by C&C Offset Printing Co., Ltd.

The authorised representative in the EEA is Penguin Random House Ireland, Morrison Chambers, 32 Nassau Street, Dublin D02 YH68.

Penguin Random House is committed to a sustainable future for our business, our readers and our planet. This book is made from Forest Stewardship Council® certified paper.